ANDRES D. HORTILLOSA

IMPROVE YOUR CHESS AT ANY AGE

EVERYMAN CHESS
www.everymanchess.com

First published in 2009 by Gloucester Publishers plc (formerly Everyman Publishers plc), Northburgh House, 10 Northburgh Street, London EC1V 0AT

British Library Cataloguing-in-Publication Data
A catalogue record for this book is available from the British Library.

ISBN: 978 1 85744 618 0

Distributed in North America by The Globe Pequot Press, P.O Box 480, 246 Goose Lane, Guilford, CT 06437-0480.

All other sales enquiries should be directed to Everyman Chess, Northburgh House, 10 Northburgh Street, London EC1V 0AT
tel: 020 7253 7887 fax: 020 7490 3708
email: info@everymanchess.com; website: www.everymanchess.com

Everyman is the registered trade mark of Random House Inc. and is used in this work under licence from Random House Inc.

Everyman Chess Series
Chief advisor: Byron Jacobs
Commissioning editor: John Emms
Assistant editor: Richard Palliser

Typeset and edited by First Rank Publishing, Brighton.
Cover design by Horatio Monteverde.
Printed and bound in the US by Versa Press.

Contents

Bibliography

Books/ebooks

Accelerated Dragons, John Donaldson & Jeremy Silman (Everyman Chess 1998)

Attacking Manual Volume 1, Jacob Aagaard (Quality Chess 2008)

Beating Unusual Chess Openings, Richard Palliser (Everyman Chess 2007)

Challenging the Nimzo-Indian, David Vigorito (Quality Chess 2007)

Dealing with d4 Deviations, John Cox (Everyman Chess 2007)

Easy Guide to the Nimzo-Indian, John Emms (Cadogan 1998)

Fighting the Anti-Sicilians, Richard Palliser (Everyman Chess 2007)

How to Reassess Your Chess, Jeremy Silman (Siles Press 1993)

Play the Semi-Slav, David Vigorito (Quality Chess 2008)

Secrets of Practical Chess, John Nunn (Gambit 1998)

Starting Out: Closed Sicilian, Richard Palliser (Everyman Chess 2007)

Starting Out: The Accelerated Dragon, Andrew Greet (Everyman Chess 2008)

Starting Out: The King's Indian Attack, John Emms (Everyman Chess 2007)

The Search for Chess Perfection, C.J.S. Purdy (Thinker's Press 1997)

The Sicilian Accelerated Dragon, P.H. Nielsen & Curt Hansen (Batsford 1998)

The Survival Guide to Competitive Chess, John Emms (Everyman Chess 2007)

Websites, Databases and Analysis Engines

Big Database 2008

Chesspublishing.com

Chessville.com

Deep Fritz 11

Deep Junior 10
Deep Rybka 3
The Week in Chess 1-761
USMilitaryChess.org

Acknowledgments

None of our notable undertakings are pursued to their happy conclusions without manifest help from beneficent souls who invade graciously our life experience. The book you are holding is no exception. It found life from the confluence of efforts by family, friends, coaches, chess opponents and honourable acquaintances. I am indebted to many in the writing of this book, but the following are foremost on the list.

Dorry, my ultra-sweet wife whose empowering encouragement and unfailing support practically nourished this book from its inception to completion. The least I could do to acknowledge her irreplaceable contribution is to dedicate this book in her honour.

Alina Grace, my six-year-old daughter and most ardent fan. Any father armed with these three fighting words in "No mercy, Daddy" has to be taken seriously over the board.

Ann Marie, my benefactor and employer for the most part of 2008. I was fortunate indeed to have an employer who graciously allowed me to take frequent vacations so I could play chess without fear of getting fired. Well, it helps a little when the employer happens to be your kid sister and a chess player.

Kelly Atkins, my editor at www.chessville.com whose generous praise and wise guidance of my columns nudged me towards a book idea.

Phil Innes, for facilitating the opportunity to write as a columnist for www.chessville.com.

David Surrat, trailblazer and visionary publisher of www.chessville.com, for his tireless dedication in helping amateurs everywhere improve at chess.

Dan Addelman, for graciously passing on the book idea to the editors at Everyman Chess. I never expected him to comply, but he did.

Grandmaster John Emms, commissioning editor at Everyman Chess, for his encouragement and patient guidance while this book grew out of labour pains. His courageous decision to publish the work of an untitled improving player truly deserves praise. In our collaboration for this work he has proven himself to be a par excellence editor.

Last but not least is my current coach, Grandmaster Dmitry Gurevich. The professionalism he demonstrates in his work as a chess teacher sees no equal but it is his gentle demeanour which fuels his sincerest desire to help improvers derive the most joy in the playing of the royal game that endears him to his students.

Introduction

When word of the book release reached the ethereal world of chess, it attracted mixed reactions from players sporting ratings close to my target threshold. Surprisingly, most encouraging remarks came from a class of players we universally regard to be de facto chess gods as proven by their achieved titles. Many snarky remarks pretentiously wrapped in serious thought came from a group of players who upon closer investigation have never achieved a rating mark equal to mine; yet they question my credentials with the ferocity not seen among stronger players.

Some unwilling to give ground to the possibility that what I am proposing deserves their impartial investigation reluctantly characterized my offered proof as luck. So, do chess players get lucky? Does this sort of thing happen to a chess player within the bounds of the sixty-four squares? Well, it depends. Luck as generally postulated manifests in chess in different forms. One instance of luck can be a simple case of an opponent losing a winning position by making a blunder. Perhaps another case involves an opponent prematurely resigning a drawn position. Be it this or that is immaterial to me, as I would rather attribute my luck to hard work echoing the words of Samuel Goldwyn when he said, "The harder I work, the luckier I get."

This notion takes significant relevance to this book because my positive result at the 2008 New England Masters, referenced on the back cover of this book as positive proof to the claims of my evolving chess thinking process, when taken as a singular event is declared by a few critics to be insufficient.

My chess thinking process which forms the core of my chess improvement plan has been proven effective by my results in four major tournaments, three of which are 9 rounds in duration.

Before proceeding further let me be clear about this important point that easily escapes the minds even of those who are intent in their desire to improve. You improve by reading almost anything. We seem to believe that most chess teachers decry the benefits of studying opening tomes. Actually, that is not what they are saying at all. What happens is that we hear some things loudly and others not so loudly. The one thing we think we hear loudly is the coaches' tendency to discredit opening books. In most cases, what they are preaching against is directed at our exclusive focus on the study of openings as the way to achieve overall chess improvement.

Anyone who studies any opening benefits by virtue of the newly-acquired knowledge on that particular opening. Our mistake is in assuming that new opening knowledge will translate positively to the overall conduct of the game. Have we forgotten the three phases that naturally divides a chess game? And yet we erroneously conclude that the highly sought improvement in the opening phase of the game will extend as well into the middlegame or ending. It sounds familiar, doesn't it? I can speak of it honestly because I too had befallen headlong in misery to this illogical assumption. We don't readily acknowledge this error to be present in our thinking but we know it is true in our experience.

So what is chess improvement? Should we rather concern ourselves with the "how" instead of the "what"? I argue that it is thus far easier to get to the "how" if we agree first on the "what" of the issue.

In this book, chess improvement will take on a different meaning in a defined construct. Chess improvement is one notion we seem to know when we see one but when forced to explain it in words, we tend to flounder. To many, chess improvement is just an abstraction of what really happens in terms of positive gains in our chess playing. To some, it is denoted and expressed in a relative number we call ratings.

The former group cares about gains in understanding measured in terms of new knowledge acquired by the learning activity. The person subscribing to this notion may have questions as follows: Is my understanding of hanging pawns better now than before? Do I understand the subtleties of double pawns, passed pawns and pawn islands more than ever? Does my reading of this opening book bring me new insights into the opening? Does my viewing of this video lecture give me a better understanding of the intricacies of the Ruy Lopez?

We know we have gained new knowledge because we simply know new things. The gains do not require evidence other than our own declaration and acceptance of the fact. To the person seeking this type of chess improvement, the evidence is seen on display during the actual playing regardless of how the outcome is scored or recorded. What is satisfying to this class of players is the quality of the struggle and not the incidental result of the struggle. I agree this notion is too idealistic even for my sentiments. I strive to play well but I like it even more if the point tallies under my name on the scoreboard.

In other words, the mere display of the gains in knowledge at the board is enough to satisfy the effaceable search for improvement. These players usually do not give high regard to how the game ended, whether it is a loss, draw or win. They find more satisfaction in the actual conduct of the struggle than on the outcome. That is not to say that outcomes are not good because they are. But it is the nature of chess that some games, despite their flawless conduct from opening to ending, can sometimes end in a draw or, even worse, in a loss spoiled by an oversight or blunder. The winning side that profits from the blunder is happy with the score but if he is serious about chess improvement should feel miserable over his conduct of the game. He knows he cannot be this lucky all the time and the wins are far sweeter if they come by his own efforts. Meanwhile, the loser finds redemption from his improved play.

The latter group cares about how the gains manifest in rating increases and rating decreases. If a player sees a decline, he concludes he is regressing not improving. When he sees an increase, he believes he is indeed improving.

I further argue that one accrues improvement each time he experiences any learning activity. Learning is achieved by reading a book, solving chess puzzles, studying a new opening, watching a video lecture and the like but more so in the mere playing of the game itself. No matter what form the learning activity shapes in, as long as something is learned that activity produces a gain in improvement. Some improvements are enormous, some are incremental and some are undeniably rapid. The sum of these improvements produces intangibles like the joy that comes with winning despite a material deficit.

I concede the point that ultimately rating increases trending upwards are the ultimate measures of chess improvement as this remains a material world immersed in pragmatism. Others have strongly argued that even in the slow but gradual rise in one's ratings we can detect some perceptible hints of improvement. But not all chess improvement is manifested by sudden or steady climb in ratings.

In fact, I will dare argue that an improving player never arrives in a philosophical sense. The improving player always seeks to further his or her gains by yet another length of measure. It should be an ongoing experience. Once a milestone is attained, another one beckons from a distance for our pursuit.

I continually declare myself to be an improving player. I even sign my name in chess forums as such. Really, the declaration itself has become not just a form of reminder but empowering words of encouragement as well in the hour of defeats. But I am also on point to dispel the foolish notion that my peak was already achieved in my younger days. My challenge for you is to bravely face the same quest. Unshackle yourself and break the chains of self-imposed limitations hampering your own chess improvement. Get rid of self-serving excuses which so far have lulled you to accept your own failings as caused by the unalterable oppression of nature we call lack of natural talent. We often mistakenly equate lack of effort with lack of talent.

Am I qualified to write such a book on chess improvement, granted that we will have defined it in an agreeable way by the end of this introduction? Well, you judge me. Let me array before you, for your unbiased perusal, my evidence.

This book targets players in the rating group under 2000 USCF or FIDE. I firmly believe this book will provide anyone with a workable blueprint to overcome the target threshold. If your rating is already over 2000, this book may be of little use to you. Still, I invite you to peruse the pages perhaps to at least encourage your own quest for loftier heights in chess.

Before you delve into the more salient aspects of the book, allow me to explain the format, structure and purpose of the book. Having these three things clarified in your mind as you read through the book is critical to getting the most from the experience.

Format

I am relying mostly on my own games from four tournaments where I judiciously applied my chess thinking process. Games by other players, mostly by grandmasters, are used as fragments to illustrate a point or explain a tactical error. I have also included games played in 1994 to give readers a window into my playing ability at the time I broke 2100 USCF.

I annotate my games with help from chess engines, specifically *Deep Rybka 3* and *Deep Fritz 11*. Any errors in analysis are my sole responsibility. John Emms provided some input in a few of the annotations, mostly clarifying some vague assessments.

Structure

The chapter headings are taken from the names of tournaments I participated in. Sections of the chapters are the instructional games I played in these tournaments. Some are wins and some are losses. They were chosen primarily for their instructional value. My discussions giving shape to my improvement plan are embedded in the annotations. Some better alternatives during the games are included only if they strengthen the point being made.

This is not a book on openings but some discussions on the subject are included to manifest my personal development in that area.

Purpose

The book disavows any claim that it will make you reach master level chess. Its only modest goal is to equip you with the right tools guided by a sensible improvement plan to help you scale the 2000 Elo wall. Its purpose is not to eliminate your blunders but to diminish their unwanted visits to an acceptable rarity where you get to play relatively good chess and pleasantly extract some joy from the experience. It is my sincerest desire to help other desiring chess players improve at chess regardless of age. It is the humble aim of this work to do exactly what the title suggests.

Andres D. Hortillosa
Minneapolis, USA
October 2009

Chapter One

My First Breakthrough Year

It's not 2008 as you might suspect. It was 1994. What happened that year is the key to understanding this book and how this so-called chess thinking process, which forms the core of my chess improvement plan, came into being. That year I saw myself playing some really good chess at least in my eyes. My USCF rating broke the 2100 mark and I was pushing for the next 100 points to reach master level but duty to country intervened.

Let me show you sample games played during this period for your fair judgment. I apologize in advance if none meets your standard for good chess.

The first specimen is taken from the Colorado Open. In this game I was paired against a strong master named Michael Ginat, who won the Colorado Closed Championship in 1992. He won two more titles in 1998 and 2001.

Game 1
A.Hortillosa-M.Ginat
Denver 1994
Torre Attack

1 d4 ♘f6 2 ♘f3 d6 3 ♗g5 ♘e4 4 ♗h4 ♘d7 5 ♘bd2 ♘df6 6 ♗xf6 ♘xf6 7 e4 g6 8 ♗e2 ♗g7 9 0-0 0-0 10 b4 c6 11 c3 ♕c7 12 ♕c2 ♗d7 13 a4 ♖ad8 14 ♖ab1 ♗c8 15 ♖fe1 e5 16 dxe5 dxe5 17 c4 a5 18 c5 axb4 19 ♖xb4 ♕a5 20 ♖b6

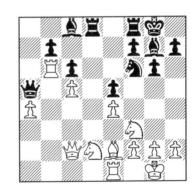

White's last move plugs the escape hatch for the queen so she can be hunted down.

20...Ⓡfe8 21 ♘b3 ♛xa4 22 ♗c4 ♛a8 23 Ⓡa1 ♛b8 24 ♘a5 ♛c7

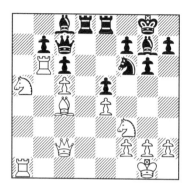

25 ♘g5

It is important to flick in the knight before crashing in on b7.

25...Ⓡf8 26 ♘xb7 ♗xb7 27 Ⓡa7 Ⓡb8 28 ♛b3

Now, White's pressure on b7 and f7 is hard to meet.

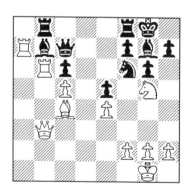

28...♛e7 29 Ⓡaxb7 Ⓡxb7 30 Ⓡxb7 ♘d7 31 ♘xf7 1-0

And seeing no active counterplay, Black resigned.

The next game was played in my only opportunity to participate in the coveted Colorado Master/Expert Class Championship. The game and annotations first appeared in an article I wrote for www.USMilitaryChess.org, and are reprinted here with permission. I did a complete revision to conform to the format of this book.

> ## Game 2
> ## A.Hortillosa-D.Hartsook
> ## Denver 1994
> ## *Torre Attack*

1 d4 ♘f6 2 ♘f3 e6 3 ♗g5 h6 4 ♗xf6

I normally do not like exchanging my dark-squared bishop for a knight early in the opening but this line is an exception. For further discussion on this line, see Hortillosa-Hungaski (Game 26).

4...♛xf6 5 e4 ♘c6

Black has other reasonable choices besides the text, such as 5...d6 or 5...g6.

6 c3 g5

To my mind this move is a little committal, although a number of strong players have used this advance. Karpov played ...g6 in one of his games, although that was without ...♘c6.

Amateurs including myself tend to make inflexible moves. We tend to forget that *pawns do not move backwards*. And once they are fixed on a square, they are subject to attack and they tend to leave you with limited options. Pay attention to what happens to the g-pawn later in the game.

7 ♗d3

Where to place pieces in the opening is one facet of the game that presents many challenges, especially to amateurs. The pawn structure arising from the opening system I employ in any game helps me to decide where to place my minor pieces and which side of the board to castle.

Playing the Torre Attack in the current game gives White a blueprint as to where the pieces should go. Growth in chess is demonstrated when one becomes aware of subtle changes in the position, as well as knowing when and how to adapt to the changes.

7...d6

Besides enforcing your plans as the focus of your efforts on the board, understanding your opponent's ideas should be your other concern. After all, two sets of ideas are at play in a struggle. While you work hard enabling your ideas to triumph, mere attempts of circumventing the opposing ideas can facilitate your own success. Strive to understand the reasoning behind your opponent's moves. If you ignore your opponent's moves, you will only understand half of the game, and in many cases it will be to your peril.

Black wants to stop e4-e5, rendering my bishop on d3 limited in scope. Should Black really need to prevent it? Can it be allowed so he can undermine it later to his advantage with ...d7-d6? Or maybe he plans to enforce ...e6-e5 himself to ensure my bishop on d3 will have nil influence along the b1-h7 diagonal.

8 ♘a3

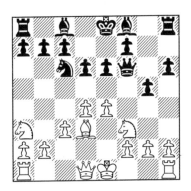

On purpose, Black has postponed his kingside development to keep me guessing where he plans to hide his king. In response, White is forced to deviate from the standard set-up. I delayed castling on the kingside so as not to give Black an open invitation for a direct attack on that side of the board.

A further point of developing the queen's knight via a3 is to free d2 for the other knight on f3 in case Black attacks it with ...g5-g4, which is a likely possibility. This flexible move also gives White the option of planting a knight on e3, via c2 or c4.

8...a6

Black is also getting ready to expand on the queenside in case I castle there. So, I answered by developing the queen:

9 ♕e2

But why e2, you asked? It is the only candidate square left since c2 and d2 are reserved squares for the knights.

9...g4

As anticipated, my opponent took the opportunity to harass the knight with tempo. I could have prevented the advance into my territory with a move like h2-h3 but I wanted him to overextend. Here is an example of allowing your opponent to carry out his idea, only to undermine it later. I reasoned that if this pawn became fixed I would be able to forcibly open the h-file.

When you can take something away from your opponent, wisely resist the urge and falsify the idea first before biting into the apple. In most cases forcing a piece to abandon its post with a pawn push is beneficial for obvious reasons. Black's strategic error comes later when he castles kingside. The overextended g-pawn and its fixed nature then becomes the open doorway into Black's castled position.

10 ♘d2 h5

As you can see the gained tempo is immediately spent because the g-pawn

needs protection from the queen on e2. Black, in return, has gained space on that side of the board. Now ...♗h6 looks inviting as the bishop on this diagonal would gain scope and would be unopposed. The queenside is certainly looking to be the obvious home for the black king.

11 ♘c2 ♗h6 12 0-0-0

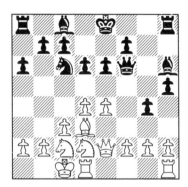

The position has become double-edged. Seeing no other useful waiting move, I decided to castle queenside. I was convinced Black would castle there as well, although Black could also keep his king in the middle and get a head start on a promising queenside attack.

12...♗d7 13 ♔b1

Played so my pinned knight on d2 can move at will. If there are no direct threats to your pieces or to squares (enemy pieces threatening to control or occupy a key square), try to improve your pieces so they are ready for deployment.

The position at this point looks equal but I like Black's chances on the kingside where he has more space.

However, the fluid situation in the middle precludes Black from immediately attacking without risking the future of his hesitant king.

13...e5

This appears a logical continuation. I would play it too if I were Black. How should White react?

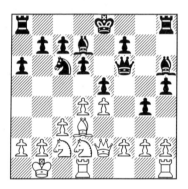

Amateurs, when confronted with situations like this one, tend to resolve tensions rather hastily. I guess amateur thinking dislikes complexity so there is a strong tendency to simplify at the first opportunity. So, it is either capture on e5 or advance to d5. I can opt to maintain the pawn on d4 with ♘db3, but it will invite Black to harass the knight on b3 with ...a6-a5-a4. Besides, the resulting position after pawns are exchanged on d4 is not good for White. It is only Black who will benefit from the resulting structure.

In general, however, one must learn to play comfortably with contact-tension on the board. Keep the tension as long as tolerable. See if you can force your opponent to waste a tempo in resolving the tension. For example, avoid capturing defenceless pawns right away. Often, a developing or centralizing move is the better choice.

14 d5 ♘e7 15 ♘c4

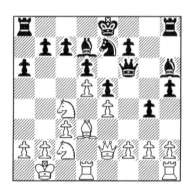

I had to play this now if I wanted to place a knight on e3, otherwise ...b7-b5 would give Black control of the c4-square. The game has evolved to look like a typical King's Indian expansion on the kingside, except here Black's king is still uncastled and Black's g-pawn is on g4 rather than g6. With this pawn structure, White benefits if he can place a knight on e3 to dissuade Black from playing ...f5.

15...♘g6

This forced me to play g2-g3, a move I was dying to play anyway to fix the g4-pawn. I wondered why he rejected chasing my knight on c4 right away, as that gains space on the queenside. But ...b5 only forces my knight to e3, where it wants to go.

Sometimes it is best to abstain from making an obvious move if that, at best, only forces your opponent to find a good defensive response. *Do not prod your opponent into finding a good move with your meaningless threats.* We often help our opponent unwittingly by doing this. Calling his attention to a weakness only eliminates his task and burden of finding the mitigation to repair it with a prophylactic move. *Some weaknesses are hard to notice until the other side highlights its existence with a positional threat.* Defer a singular threat until one becomes two, thereby gaining in potency. It is when faced by a combination of threats that your opponent will be unable to find a good defensive response.

16 g3

Eagerly played, preventing the ...♘f4 intrusion and also fixing the g4-pawn. But I was unhappy with my position because all the chances seem to belong to Black especially if he does not castle. He alone can play on both wings. I resigned myself to the sad prospect of waiting for his attack.

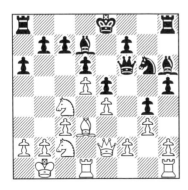

16...♖b8

Lo and behold, here he comes. But

then I thought an imminent opening of the f-file would harass his vulnerable queen and the file itself could serve as an unobstructed avenue of counterplay. My next move was designed to facilitate the opening of the f-file.

17 ♖df1

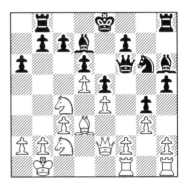

Rybka and *Fritz* adjudge the position to be still equal after this move.

17...0-0?

I could not believe that my opponent had castled into a possible attack. I got excited, of course.

My attack developed swiftly because my pieces were positioned ready for an invasion on that sector of the board. Perhaps the danger did not look obvious to Black because my piece placements were not visibly directed for such an attack. It would seem that I carefully masked my intentions, but the reality could not be farther from this. In truth, my unsuspecting opponent simply made a strategic error.

18 ♘4e3

With the rook on f1, I am ready to open the file with f2-f3 next move.

Black has no time to pin my rook after it recaptures on f3 with ...♝g4 as his undefended queen on f6 needs a tempo to evacuate from the line of fire emanating from the rook.

18...♛e7?

This is a mistake as it gives me the opportunity to continue with my next move.

Be alert for new possibilities; inflexibility can be ruinous because it inhibits creativity. Be careful to check, however, that the perceived "new" possibilities are indeed superior to the original plan. Otherwise, distractions can be dangerous.

19 ♘f5 ♛g5!?

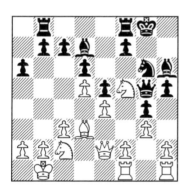

Interesting. I took some time to discover Black's real intentions with this move. At first glance, it looks like he simply wishes to protect the bishop on h6. *It helps to ask, what else does he want?*

20 ♘ce3

This move was a delight to make because it gave the impression that I would recapture with this knight if

Black took the other knight on f5. Its real purpose is to prevent Black from bailing out by threatening the exchange of queens with ...♛d2. Sneaky, I thought. I was proud of my effort finding this possibility over the board. The exchange of queens could potentially spoil or at the very least diminish the number of forces for the gathering onslaught.

20...♝xf5

Well, the subterfuge worked. What should White recapture with on f5? Maintaining an imposing knight on f5 looks very threatening.

Fundamental to your chess development is deciding when to quicken your pace and when to slow down. Double checking even generally accepted good moves, like planting a knight on f5, against concrete lines should never be taken for granted. So, what is wrong with the knight recapture?

Let's put up a diagram to see some obvious and subtle differences after 21 ♘xf5.

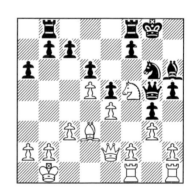

Limiting our observations to the static nature of the position, we see the knight projecting power and terror into the heart of Black's enclave. It controls crucial squares around the king and restricts enemy forces.

Black can try exchanging queens on d2 with 21...♕d2 when White has several choices including taking the bishop on h6 with the knight to avoid the queen exchange: 22 ♘xh6+ ♕xh6 23 h3 ♕g5 24 hxg4 hxg4.

Comparing the quality of the remaining pieces on the board reveals that the bishop on d3 is "bad" because of its limited scope, whereas Black's knight on g6 protects the invasion point of attack on h8. With the back king moving up to g7, a rook can then challenge White's forces on the h-file. White's advantage here is minimal when compared to the other lines. If you remove all the major pieces, Black's position would look tenable were it not for the weak g-pawn.

Positional considerations seem to suggest that exchanging the knight for the bishop even on g7 is not a preferable trade. Since it is Black's turn he can dictate the terms as to where this exchange would occur. Let's just say Black wants the exchange to occur on g7 so he retreats the bishop with the move 21...♗g7. Play might then continue with the sequence 22 h3 ♖fe8 23 hxg4 hxg4 24 ♖h2 ♘e7 25 ♖fh1 ♘xf5 26 exf5.

In this line, White comes out better and may eventually nurse his advantage to a conclusive win. Because of White's dominance on the open file, the weak g-pawn will fall. Meanwhile, Black is slow with his counterplay on the queenside.

21 exf5

I might have said in my head, "Sorry, just kidding. I really wanted to occupy f5 with a pawn." This is where the correct evaluation of the position pays its worth. In many cases, concrete variations, not biases, are compulsory in establishing the validity of choices and the veracity of their respective claims.

Rybka gives White a decisive edge with my choice of capturing with a pawn. My reasoning for choosing the text move was simple: I wanted to force Black to waste a tempo in saving the knight so I could immediately play the advance h2-h3 with the intent of capturing on g4 and continuing with ♖h4 pressuring the g-pawn after Black recaptures.

21...♞e7

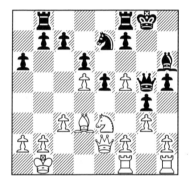

Be careful where you place your pieces because they may reduce the number of escape squares for your most valuable piece, for example Black's queen in this game. When you only have one safe square for your queen when threatened, the situation is almost always dire.

An interesting try for Black is 21...e4, when play might continue 22 ♗c2 ♞e5 23 h3 with White pressing his attack. The winning plan, as with the other lines, begins with this file-opening move.

22 h3

So what exactly is the winning plan? Here is one example of a position where the need to calculate concrete variations, while still very much preferred, has become less necessary. The move h2-h3 invites itself. This is a type of position where intuition or "feel" proves usable. You just know that some moves are intrinsically good.

Note that f2-f3 as a lever candidate is no longer possible because the knight on e3 would hang.

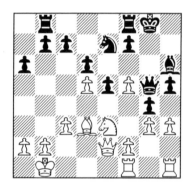

22...♗g7

The bishop hopes to replace the wandering g-pawn as shield to the insecure king.

23 hxg4 hxg4 24 ♖h4

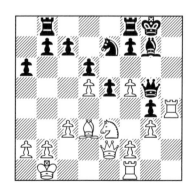

The fixed g-pawn is Black's undoing in this game. The rest is easy.

24...c6

Black's last gasp for counterplay but it is too late.

25 ♖xg4 ♕f6 26 ♖h4 cxd5 27 ♕h5 ♕h6 28 ♕g4 1-0

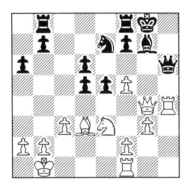

Finding good moves becomes easier when your pieces are harmoniously placed and when your structure is positionally sound. I like 28 ♕g4 because it pins the bishop on g7 and disallows its ability to capture a checking rook on h8. Seeing the inevitability of ♖fh1 and the indefensible mate on h8, Black gave up. Even now, I consider this to be one of my satisfying games. It is hard to believe it was over in less than 30 moves.

The next three examples were all played at the 1994 National Open, in Las Vegas. This year's edition was won by GM Grigory Kaidanov. In the first encounter, I was totally winning but because of an incorrect sequence of moves suffered a heart-breaking loss. You will see why.

Game 3
A.Hortillosa-D.Strenzwilk
National Open,
Las Vegas 1994
Torre Attack

1 d4 g6 2 ♘f3 ♗g7 3 c3 d6 4 ♗g5 ♘f6 5 ♘bd2 h6 6 ♗xf6 ♗xf6 7 e4 0-0 8 ♗e2 c5 9 dxc5 dxc5 10 0-0 ♘c6 11 ♕c2 ♕c7 12 h3 ♖b8 13 a4 a6 14 ♘c4 b5 15 axb5 axb5 16 ♘e3 e6 17 ♘g4 ♗g7 18 ♕d2 ♔h7 19 ♕e3 f5 20 exf5 exf5 21 ♘gh2 ♕b6 22 ♖fd1 b4 23 ♖d6

White is targeting the weak g6-square.

23...♗b7 24 ♘h4 ♖be8 25 ♕g3 g5 26 ♗d3 gxh4 27 ♕g6+ ♔h8

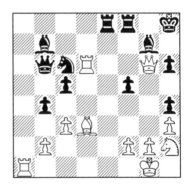

This is one of the few critical points in the game, and therefore I should have taken more time before continuing. But without doing proper reconnaissance of the new position, I recklessly continued with the plan hatched earlier on move 23.

Always invest time to update your plan because the last-played move usu-

ally changes the battle terrain, which may require a slight or drastic change in the plan. Neglecting to update the plan may lead to missing out on better opportunities on the board, to say the least. There are cases where failure to update the plan as necessitated by the structural changes may even lead to defeat as in this game. Some defeats are wrought not by your opponent's strong moves, but by your own weak moves. Exercise vigilance in curbing your tendencies for autopilot moves. We seem to have a strong propensity for unexamined moves, precipitated either by laziness or overestimation of our chances or underestimation of opponent's resources, but even more so by unbridled momentum.

On my next move, I played what I thought was just crushing and stood ready to accept Black's resignation.

28 ♗xf5??

Had I applied the system on the current position while asking the key question, "Do I have something better that is more forcing than the one I intend?" I would have seen that 28 ♖d7! was a better alternative which would win on the spot as Black has no defence to the threat against the bishop on g7.

(see following diagram)

If Black defends the threat with 28...♖g8 then 29 ♗xf5 yields the unstoppable mate threat on h7. Another defensive try for Black is to obstruct the rook's attack path to g7 with either 28...♘e7 or 28...♖e7.

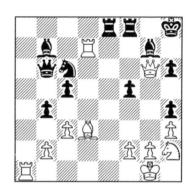

However, neither saves the game because both choices would leave the queen on b6 hanging (the latter after 29 ♖xe7 ♘xe7).

Because I did not use the system, I chose a less forcing move and wrongly executed the sequence. Instead of resignation, a defiant reply appeared on the board in the form of an exchange sacrifice. *Always consider all legal captures as defensive possibilities.*

28...♖xf5

The move sent a chill up my spine and both ears started to feel awfully warm from the rushing blood. I slowly realized that I had chosen the wrong continuation.

When winning opportunities are missed, we often have to expend valuable energies dealing with the damage to the playing psyche. *But you should always take the time to settle the jarring effect to the mind otherwise the continuing moves will be fired as from a disturbed and hazy gun scope.* The sudden turn of events was such a big emotional letdown, that it caused me to treat a slightly advantageous position like a lost position. In just a few moves, my game transformed from a won game into a lost game:

29 ♕xe8+ ♖f8 30 ♕g6 ♕c7 31 ♘g4 ♕f7

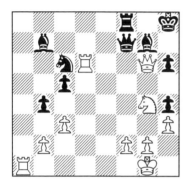

The mind, unwilling to accept the drastic change in fortunes, rejected a bailout that would preserve the slight advantage and instead played a blunder which turned the tables in Black's favour. I recklessly avoided the exchange of queens on f7 and played **32 ♕d3?**, which promptly elicited the crushing reply **32...♘e5**.

At this point, I was lumbering in a daze and resigned the game in disgust three moves later: **33 ♕e3 ♘c4 34 ♘xh6 ♕h5 35 ♘f7+ 0-1**.

The second game from this tournament is against Arizona master Steve Stubenrauch.

> ### Game 4
> ### S.Stubenrauch-A.Hortillosa
> ### National Open,
> ### Las Vegas 1994
> ### *Torre Attack*

1 ♘f3 d5 2 d4 ♘f6 3 ♗g5 ♗f5 4 e3 ♘bd7 5 ♗d3 ♗xd3 6 ♕xd3 c5 7 ♘bd2 c4 8 ♕e2 e6 9 e4 ♗e7 10 e5 ♘g8 11 ♗f4 g5 12 ♗e3 h5 13 c3 ♖c8 14 0-0 ♘h6 15 ♘e1 ♘f5 16 ♘c2 ♘f8 17 ♖ab1 ♘g6 18 b3 cxb3 19 ♖xb3 b6 20 a4 ♘f4 21 ♗xf4 gxf4 22 ♖a1 ♘h4 23 ♘e1 ♕c7 24 a5 ♗d8 25 axb6 axb6 26 ♔f1 ♕e7 27 ♕a6 ♖b8 28 ♕b5+ ♔f8 29 ♖ba3 ♕g5 30 ♖a8 ♖xa8 31 ♖xa8 ♔g7 32 ♕d7 f3 33 ♘dxf3 ♘xf3 34 gxf3

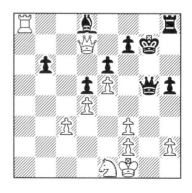

34 ♘xf3 would lead to a draw but White wanted more.

34...♖g8 35 ♖a7

White missed a tactical stroke in 35 f4!, forcing Black's queen to stay on the diagonal to avoid losing the bishop on d8. 35...♕e7 and 35...♕h4 would be the only options.

35...♕g6

35...♕f5 gives Black more options including a check on h3.

36 ♖b7 ♗h4 37 ♕b5?

White wants to protect the light squares, specifically b1 and d3, from the black queen so he can drive the bishop on h4 away with ♘g2. The idea is quietly refuted by Black's next move:

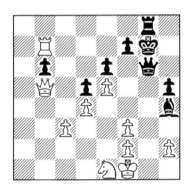

37...♔h6

Black's king is now much safer than its uncovered counterpart.

38 ♔e2 ♕g1 39 ♘d3

With the text move, White is hoping to slow down Black's attack a bit so he can engineer his own attack starting with ♖xf7.

39...♗xf2

Suddenly, White's king is facing mortal danger. Undeterred by my aggression, my opponent keeps on fighting with his next move.

40 ♖xf7 ♗h4

White was likely banking on ♖f6+ to either give him a win or at least a perpetual.

But this nice retreat is what White overlooked. Black protects against ♖f6+ and prepares ...♖g2+, which is totally winning. *Retreating moves are harder to see than advancing moves, especially those made by the attacking side.*

Let's see what happens if Black ignores the possible check on f6 and instead plays the gross blunder 40...♕xh2. After 41 ♖f6+ ♔g5 42 ♘xf2, White is the one who is grinning.

41 ♘f4 ♕f2+ 42 ♔d3 ♕f1+

This nasty check forces the knight to abandon its defence of g2, allowing the rook occupation of that square. The rest of the moves are almost forced.

43 ♘e2 ♖g2 44 ♔d2 ♕e1+ 45 ♔e3 ♗f2+ 46 ♔f4 ♕d2 mate (0-1)

My opponent actually allowed the mate to occur on the board.

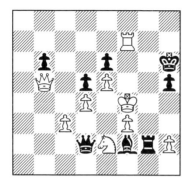

My opponent in the third round was rated Expert by USCF. He improved rapidly in the subsequent years following this clash and soon became a FIDE Master.

Game 5
D.Roper-A.Hortillosa
National Open,
Las Vegas 1994
Sicilian Defence

1 e4 c5 2 c3 ♘c6 3 d4 cxd4 4 cxd4 g6 5 ♘c3 ♗g7 6 ♗e3 e6 7 ♘f3

Necessary now is 7...d5 to keep the balance.

7...♘ge7 8 d5 exd5 9 exd5 ♘b4 10 ♗c4

Much better for White is 10 ♕b3 ♕a5 11 d6 giving him the advantage.

10...♕c7?

What is wrong with this move? Can something be wrong with the move when it develops and threatens the bishop on c4? It has got to be good, and I thought so until I looked a little deeper. My opponent simply believed

my lie. *Do not trust your opponent's version of the truth on the board. You must do your own fact-checking.*

11 ♕b3?

What was good one move earlier no longer suffices here as the position has changed. Be wary of second chances to play seemingly good moves without another look.

A strong refutation if White had taken more time is 11 ♘b5 since 11...♕a5 12 ♗d2 will likely cost Black one of his knights.

11...♘c2+

Necessity rescues the wayward knight. As before, necessity plus effort is shown to deliver when it comes to finding good moves.

12 ♕xc2 ♕xc4 13 0-0-0

Since White cannot castle short immediately, he did what looks natural, but without a c-pawn to blunt the bishop along the diagonal it looks too dangerous. An alternative worth considering is 13 ♘d2 to drive the queen off the diagonal so that White can castle short next.

13...d6 14 ♗g5

A threat. This looks very playable as it appears to prevent Black from castling into safety because the knight would hang. How should we react to a threat? Of course, we find a bigger threat of our own. Black's forceful response seizes the initiative and the advantage. I would prefer 14 ♗d4 or even 14 ♕e4 if I were handling White.

14...♗f5

15 ♕d2

Another inaccuracy; errors tend to come in bunches. The preferable 15 ♕b3 keeps the fight going.

15...♖c8

Black ignores the attack on the knight with yet another threat, this time against a2 and by extension the king. Black is clearly in control now.

16 ♘d4 ♕xa2 17 ♘c2

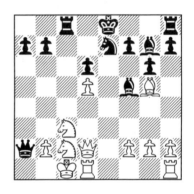

17...♕b3

A prettier line is the immediate capture on c3 with 17...♖xc3 18 bxc3 0-0 19 ♗xe7 ♗h6 20 ♗g5 ♗xg5 21 f4 ♗xf4.

18 ♖he1

His last move hopes to distract Black into defending the uneasy knight. Seeing that it cannot help in the attack, Black abandons it and castles to bring the sulking rook to the party.

18...0-0 19 ♖xe7 ♗xc3 20 bxc3 ♖xc3

It is hopeless. White resigned two moves later:

21 ♕xc3 ♕xc3 22 ♖d2 ♖c8 0-1

At the 1994 Colorado Open, after the results were tallied, I was declared winner of the Colorado Chess Tour, Overall category for the 1993-94 season. Winning is based on your tournament results for the given year starting with the Colorado Open in September 1993 and ending with some designated event in August 1994. Past winners include nationally known players like GM Alex Fishbein and IM Michael Mulyar, a former Samford Fellowship winner. Besides the small cash prize, I earned a berth to the 1995 Colorado Closed Championship, which I sadly forfeited when duty to country intervened.

My chess playing days suddenly came to an abrupt stop in 1995 when the US Army sent me to a one-year deployment in South Korea. The only chess I played that year was the All-Army Chess Championship and the NATO Chess Championship in Gausdal, Norway. Upon my return to the US mainland in February 1996, I went to graduate school for a Computer Science degree with a major in Software Engineering. It was there that I became acquainted with the little-known discipline of Cleanroom Software Engineering. Later, this software creation philosophy played an influential part in the development of my chess thinking process.

Barely two years after completing the Computer Science degree, I competed for yet another graduate program sponsored and paid for by the US Army Medical Department. I was one of the first lucky four soldier-medics chosen for the Master of Healthcare Administration program. I graduated with a Master of Business Administration degree from the University of Colorado in the summer of 2001. It was at the business school where I got acquainted with yet another influential philosophy called Six-Sigma. Both of these concepts were influential in the birthing of my chess thinking process.

So, what is the point of all these? Well, for one I want to impress a notion in the reader's mind about the dangers of chess inactivity. Because of my back-to-back graduate degrees for which I have no iota of regrets, I had a very limited number of chess games during these years. If there is one standout I can blame for my decline in abilities followed by a steady decline in ratings, it is my inactivity. Did I keep accumulating chess knowledge during this period? Yes, I did. In fact, I collected most of my chess library during this period. No doubt chess knowledge increased but the chess skill deteriorated. Short absences from the board can be healthy but long ones can imperil the chess mind to the dangers of atrophy. It was not until the second half of 2007 that I began to play tournament chess with notable frequency.

Yes, it is indeed possible; in fact, it is inevitable that you suffer a net loss in chess skills while you accrue a net gain in chess knowledge. Strange but true and knowing the difference will help you in your own escape from chess regression to chess improvement. The rest of the book will show you how.

Chapter Two

2008: The Birth of the Thinking Process

As the title suggests, 2008 was a momentous chess year for me. It marked the beginning of my return to tournament chess in a regimented way but without stifling creativity. Even my opening choices are chosen with less random influence and are no longer dependent on mood. Central to this change is my chess thinking process which is now broken down into a series of formal but repeatable process steps.

After my retirement in 2007, I suddenly found time for a lot interests put on hold while in the service. Amicable sibling diplomacy landed me a job as President of a small start-up and privately-held company. This pioneering company is the brainchild of my younger sister, Ann Marie, who currently attends the Owner/President Management (OPM) program at the Harvard Business School. Being used to multiple hats in the service, it did not faze me a bit when assigned other responsibilities as Chief Information Officer and Vice President of NC Staffing, a medical staffing agency based in Little Rock also founded by my entrepreneurial sister, which is the parent company of the start-up.

One of the job perks is the ability to take frequent vacations to play chess. However, I was unhappy almost to the point of disgust with my chess experience since 1994. One day while introspectively reflecting on the sorry affairs of my chess skills, a light bulb lit up. I wondered if I could do what in management is known as a technology transfer. Specifically, I wanted to explore the possibility of harnessing what I know in my professional trade and apply those which I affirm to be universally applicable principles into chess. Some notable masters of the game have written avowedly about the merits of chess principles in business and in life. I have always suspected the analogy to be the case of "the cart before the horse". In a way, I took exactly the opposite approach.

After this reflection, I concluded that my chess was totally devoid of any semblance of a thinking process. As it were, my move selection routine, my methods of acquiring chess knowledge, my tournament preparation regimen could be described as ad hoc. It was ironic that I lacked a logical process for a purportedly logical activity. Does it sound like you? It was just a matter of time for my penchant for process improvement to cross over into my chess. The imminent fusion of the two interests was meant to coalesce since I am known everywhere to be an avid process guy. In my mind every human activity as mundane as doing laundry, stacking a refrigerator and the like, no matter how simple, can be broken down into process steps.

Even gourmet cooking as an art form follows a well-guarded recipe. Any process step is a valid candidate for improvement as none ever reaches a state of perfection. I am passionately drawn to fixing things including those that work to make them even better. It was not hard to see my chess requiring more than just cosmetic repair; it needed total replacement.

Disgusted with the status quo, I formulated a chess thinking process inspired by the combined philosophies of Cleanroom Software Engineering and Six-Sigma, which are known for their strong emphasis on error prevention. My chess thinking process is making a bold claim that it will help any player improve regardless of age. By extension, it will capacitate the disciplined practitioner of the process secure lasting chess improvement. And with the improvement, as it is in my experience, there comes the desired benefit of fully enjoying the game in its better form where you are on the winning side more often.

The chess thinking process I am about to share with you is a product of deliberate thought. So far, it has proven its efficacy on more than one occasion. The rest of the story is yet to be told in the near future as the process continues to evolve towards maturity. A disciplined and rigorous application of the process in every game over time will make its use less of a conscious act. The goal is to assimilate the process until it becomes more of a subconscious act. When I reach that level of competence, it will enable me to scale the ELO summit of 2200. I sincerely wish your improvement efforts will be richly rewarded as well.

Let me now describe to you what this process is in this chapter, and then I will offer for your examination a body of evidentiary facts arguing for its effectiveness in the remainder of the book. My initial foray into the playgrounds ruled by the big boys in events like the 2008 New England Masters, the 2008

Pan-American Continental Championship, the 2009 Mid-America Open and the 19th North American FIDE Invitational have secured for the process positive proof of its veracity and efficacy, and these events are dealt with at length in their own separate chapters.

Tactics: A New Approach

First, let's consider some relevant issues necessary to frame our discussion within a defined context. The bulk of the ideas in this chapter first saw light in a column I wrote for www.chessville.com. Some of the ideas were revised, extended and expanded for the book. Most of the illustrative games were all played in the second half of 2008 and the first half of 2009.

Tactics as a subset of chess are either overly emphasized or detrimentally ignored by players below master level. We all seem to agree that the mastery of chess tactics finds its utmost expression in the practical demonstration of tactical skills in actual games. A high score denoting proficiency obtained from a tactics server or a similar tool is meaningless to us if it does not translate to positive results in our games. With regards to the plurality of methods we employ in the acquisition and sharpening of tactical skills, the list abounds in proportion to differing philosophies found in literature to date. But what is lost often in philosophical discussions on the very subject of chess ability and improvement is the

fact that tactical skill by its nature like any other skills can be acquired, developed and sharpened.

Only a handful of chess writers truly understand the best method of acquiring tactical skills. Most authors believe, as evidenced by the books and software available on the market, the repetitive solving of puzzle exercises is the best approach to developing tactical skills. In my view, *the best way to learn tactics for players below master level is to actually play over the moves leading to the staging point of the puzzle.* The staging point for our purposes is simply the initial diagrammed position of the puzzle.

For us, the key learning event is not in the finding of the solution to the puzzle but in the knowing of how to set up the conditions leading to a given position where a tactical combination exists. In others words, the learning benefit is greater to us if we know the specifics of constructing a mating net than finding the mate itself. By extension, we benefit more by knowing how to construct a dual attack, a skewer and a fork than the actual execution of these attacks. The master is better at disguising or staging the preconditions to these attacks than us. Our goal then is to reach parity with the master in this area as the way to improve. *Anyone can solve a puzzle, but can anyone play the moves leading to the puzzle?*

Let's look at some examples:

In this position, between two grandmasters from the world's elite, Black has just played 52...♖a8-e8 confining the white king and limiting his movement to only two squares. Black is clearly lost, but playing on will not make him any more lost so he sets up a clever swindle starting with the text move. This is an example of an active staging of a tactical opportunity. Black is working towards a specific configuration involving the combined powers of the rook and knight in the construction of a mating net. Watch him camouflage his intent and craftily orchestrate his deception culminating in one of the biggest swindles of 2009:

53 b5

White responds by pushing his passed pawn onward to coronation while cleverly protecting the e1-square,

a potential invasion point for the rook.

53...♘h1+

Black continues with his sinister plans with the decoy check, forcing White's king away from the e3-square now that the e1-square is not available to him.

54 ♔g1

White happily obliges and attacks the knight on h1. So, now what?

54...♖e3

After this move White is facing the practical problem of how to defend the attacked bishop presently and the a3-pawn subsequently. Of a more serious concern to him is how to simultaneously defend the e1-square and the bishop. If White defends the bishop with 55 ♖d2, Black wins material starting with 55...♖e1+ followed by 56...♘g3. Now you see why White chooses the text move:

55 ♗c4

White decides to offer Black two choices: a bishop trade or the a-pawn. Mind you, this is not the blunder.

55...♖xa3

When under attack, if you have a choice of different captures, capture first the piece that has a potential for furthering your opponent's mating ambitions.

White has a choice between capturing the bishop or the knight. The square vulnerable to threats by the bishop near the white king is g2, but this square is sufficiently protected by the rook. The knight is a different story, especially when it becomes a protected piece around the king. A knight firmly planted on g3 will condemn the rook to the defence of the first rank. Based on the above considerations, the piece posing the greatest threat to the king is the knight and not the bishop. Therefore, it is the default choice for capture.

56 ♗xd5??

This is the losing blunder based on a faulty assumption involving move sequence. White is temporarily up a bishop and a pawn but he is dead lost because mate takes precedence over material superiority.

I think White incorrectly assumed

that Black had to play ...♘g3 first before he could threaten mate, for which White had ♖a2 defending against both the mate and the threat to the bishop on a5. Well, Black is not after setting up a mate threat because there is already one. The rook which was originally on a8 finally reaches a1 via the most improbable route aided by deception and trickery. This is just one more compelling proof that creativity fuelled by tenacity sees no limit in chess.

56...♖a1+ 57 ♔h2

The accidental location of the knight means the f2-square is covered so the king is forced to step onto the execution square. Next we see the killer follow-up. This is the kind of deceptive staging skill we ought to be acquiring and sharpening if we want to get very far in chess.

57...♘g3 0-1

Seeing that the mate couldn't be averted, Svidler resigned. We can only imagine the elation of triumph Gelfand felt after completing his miracle save and creative effort.

Game 7
N.Zdebskaja-A.Shneider
Cappelle la Grande 2009
Sicilian Defence

1 e4 c5 2 ♘f3 d6 3 d4 cxd4 4 ♘xd4 ♘f6 5 ♘c3 a6 6 ♗e2 e5 7 ♘b3 ♗e7 8 0-0 ♗e6 9 f4 ♕c7 10 ♔h1 0-0 11 f5 ♗c4 12 g4 d5 13 g5 ♘xe4 14 ♘xe4 dxe4 15 f6 ♗d6 16 ♗xc4 ♕xc4 17 ♗e3 ♖d8 18 fxg7 ♘c6 19 ♘d2 ♕d5 20 c4

The simple idea of this little move is to nudge the queen away from its defence of the sensitive f7-pawn. This is what we call a diversion tactic. Black can defend f7 with 20...♕e6 but this surrenders to White a juicy square for her knight after 21 ♘xe4.

20...♕d3 21 ♕g4

A promising attack on f7 appears with this move at the expense of the bishop on e3, an idea I suspect the Ukrainian grandmaster playing Black simply overlooked. To White's credit, she judged correctly that the threat to the bishop could be ignored by pursu-

ing her own threat. If she had spent a tempo on defending the bishop, then Black's decision to abandon the defence of f7, informed or not, would have been justified. Now, Black's queen has no direct path back to the defence of f7 and the king.

We can avoid similar situations if we always ask this question: *Can my opponent ignore my threat with a bigger threat?*

21...♕xe3 22 ♕f5

This is the move that justified White's sacrifice of the bishop one move ago. Black is forced to take on g7 as the threat to f7 is hard to meet by other means.

22...♔xg7 23 ♕xf7+

White must have this position in mind as a bailout in case she cannot find something else that wins once she gets here. Black is the higher rated player here, and if White is happy with a draw now, she gets it at will (with perpetual check on f7 and f6).

Against stronger opponents, or in situations where a draw isn't undesirable, it is a good idea to search for a bailout in cases where the surety of the combination is unclear due to its complexity. Some complex positions are simply beyond our calculating skills to ascertain the objective truth when deciding on a combination. But having a bailout gives us a practical reason to muster all courage for a combination. It saves time on the clock and serves as insurance. The upside is that in most cases the winning continuation usually becomes much clearer once you get to the bailout position. This suggests a practical rule that in complex positions, *it is not always necessary to know all the information before embarking on a combination.* This is not the same as going by intuition.

23...♔h8 24 ♕f6+ ♔g8

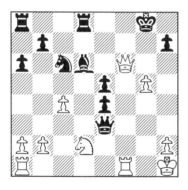

Here White sees that indeed there is a win. With fewer pieces in the vicinity of the king, the task of finding the winning continuation has gotten simpler. Any average player should easily find the path to victory. The following is a practical and effective method of creat-

ing a mating net:

25 ♕e6+ ♔h8 26 ♖f7

White is threatening 27 ♕f6+ or 27 ♕h6, depending on how Black defends.

26...♕xg5 27 ♖g1

This obvious move removes the only active defender of Black's vulnerable squares. Essentially, Black is defending his king with just one piece, the queen. White, on the other hand, is attacking with her queen and two rooks. A material imbalance like this almost always decisively favours the attacker.

27...♕xg1+ 28 ♔xg1 1-0

Seeing that he couldn't adequately defend the two mating squares on g7 and h7, Black resigned.

It is easy for one to solve puzzles of the kind that goes "Black to play and mate in three moves". This sort of presentation artificially aids the learner in finding the solution. Not only is the solver told which side wins, but he is told as well that it can be done in three moves. Knowing the number of moves it takes to mate is a key clue, which aids the brain to generate possible solutions in the solving process. And knowing which side has the edge eliminates an important learning opportunity to find the obvious and discern the nuances of the given position. This skill ought to be developed among improvers as an essential aspect of learning tactics.

The mainstream approach to tactical learning, in my estimation, is partially flawed because it tends to develop only the skill of finding tactical solutions, but not more. The skill with the most practical value during a chess game is the one that helps players recognize that a tactical opportunity exists on the board. This other skill is duly ignored by mainstream writers. An improving player needs to master foremost how to spot tactical opportunities and only then should he proceed to work out the details of the tactical solutions. This writer places a strong delineation between the two skills and argues strongly for the preference of the latter.

One utilitarian technique of finding mates in puzzles or actual games is to solve it the Filipino way. This approach to problem solving, pervasive among peoples of Oriental extraction, starts with the solution and works backwards to the problem statement. First, let's delineate "solving" from "finding" mates. Solving a mate in a puzzle is a little different from finding a mate in a real game. The end result is the same but the construct presents subtle differences.

Inherent in a puzzle is the assumption of a solution. Standard puzzles announce whose side is mating or winning. When we encounter difficulties in solving puzzles, we do not easily give up. We know we just have to strive harder if we insist in solving them. Knowing which side is winning or mating is half the answer, and that fact alone encourages us to continue searching for the answer. In a real game, it is far more challenging. In amateur games where positions are unclear and material count is equal, often combatants have no inkling as to which side is winning. Even worse is the failure on both sides to notice winning or mating opportunities. Even grandmasters occasionally have fallen victim to this malady.

The suggested technique helps you find the mate quicker because it gives you clues on how to proceed. First, imagine or ascertain where the mate occurs, specifically on which square. I say "imagine" because in rare cases it requires imagination in finding the square. I also say "ascertain" because working with the right square also means you are working on the right answer. Imagine the loss of time chasing a solution to a mystery based on flawed clues. It can get very disconcerting. It soils your memory cache with bad data and it fogs your brain with useless information. There is no software daemon in the brain that can filter this useless data out giving you a cleaner slate to work on.

When I use this technique with students, I would normally ask them to pick up literally the mating piece and drop it on the mating square. Lifting the piece off the board helps when the mating piece comes from the other side of the board. You do not want to saddle the brain with the details of how the piece gets to the mating square yet. It is easier when the mating piece is in the vicinity of the enemy king.

Second, mentally trace candidate paths of the mating piece from its current position to the mating square. It answers the question, how can it get to the mating square? Sometimes, it involves clearing pieces or exchanging defenders off the path. Sometimes, it involves correct sequencing of moves. Of course, in some instances the path determination process can get very complex. But it is in complexity where you get to behold the beauty of chess as an art form created by the interactions of these activities.

For the difficult puzzles, first find a mating motif that applies to the position. Once the motif is identified, work out the specifics of constructing the motif into form given the presence of other pieces and other realities on the board: for example, the mating side also fending off a mating attack or immediate loss of material. This is not a place for hunches; only concrete

variations are allowed. The solver often is required to find the most forcing lines in reaching his prize.

When it comes to spotting and exploiting these tactical opportunities, titled players generally demonstrate alertness and superb precision in this regard. Some opportunities are not the product of painstaking labour but they appear on the board as blunders. Even the elite of grandmasters commit blunders too. The difference is in the infrequency of occurrence.

Game 8
Y.Shulman-L.Van Wely
Foxwoods Open,
Ledyard 2009

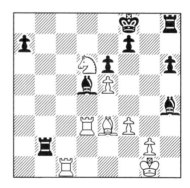

White has just played 27 ♖f1-c1. A reconnaissance of the position yields White's direct plan of invading on c7 or c8 with advantage so protecting those squares should be a priority for Black. A move like 27...♗d8 naturally comes to mind, and here 28 ♗xa7 ♖g8 29 ♗f2

looks equal. But 27...♗d8 probably looked too passive for Van Wely's taste, and he chose:

27...♗g3?

We can see why Van Wely played this move, as it attacks the pawn on e5 and prevents the white rook from moving up the board without compromising White's back rank. How should White continue?

28 ♖xd5!

Instead of defending e5, the 2008 US Champion interjects this move so he can deliver his own bigger threat after Black recaptures.

28...exd5 29 ♘f5

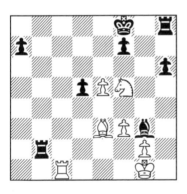

Now, it is White who threatens mate on Black's back rank with 30 ♖c8. Meanwhile, the knight performs the double function of sealing the escape squares for the black king and attacking the undefended bishop on g3. Black cannot prevent the loss of his bishop.

29...♔e8 30 ♘xg3

After this capture, Black is behind on material and resigned in two moves.

30...♔d7 31 ♗d4 ♖bb8 32 ♖a1 1-0

Here's a more straightforward example:

Game 9
J.Friedel-J.Ehlvest
US Championship,
Saint Louis 2009

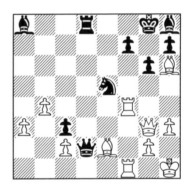

Black's last move was 33...♕d5-d2, attacking the bishop and the c2-pawn. Do a quick reconnaissance to understand the position. I think Black was hoping that White would continue with 34 ♗d1 so he could play 34...♗g7. If you were White, how would you continue?

34 ♖d1!

Black's threats are ignored and White's response exploits Black's weak back rank. Black is forced to give up his queen for the rook and bishop.

34...♕xd1+ 35 ♗xd1 ♖xd1+ 36 ♔h2 ♘c6 37 ♖e4

Black was threatening ...♗e5 so White prevents it and threatens mate with ♖e8+, which forces the return of the rook to protect its back rank.

37...♖d8 38 ♕e3 1-0

Black resigned as mate was inevitable.

Given a typical position with equal material, oftener than not, the learner does not know which side is winning. This lack of knowing is more pronounced in unbalanced positions. This is so because the learner lacks a formalized system of spotting tactical opportunities. In many amateur games, neither player receives a cue that a tactical opportunity has just materialized.

It is not unusual for some of these tactical shots to go unnoticed by both players simply because neither player was prompted to search for them during the thinking process. What is lacking is not the capacity to see it, but a system forcing the players to first look for this type of move at every turn. Loading your games for engine analysis will quickly reveal some of these missed opportunities. For sure, you will find yourself wondering how you could miss the win. The key to answering this incomprehensible flaw in our game is less of the "how" but more of the "why".

Finding one-move resources which could have changed the outcome from a loss to a win during post-mortem analysis is commonplace, even in grandmaster games. Chess engines are the ultimate finders of tactical oversights overlooked by both players during the contest. One example with grandmaster pedigree is a game between Greek GM Stelios Halkias and the 2008 World Junior Champion, Egyptian GM Ahmed Adly, which ended in a draw when it could have easily tilted towards the black corner had he noticed the blunder.

Game 10
S.Halkias-A.Adly
Reykjavik 2008

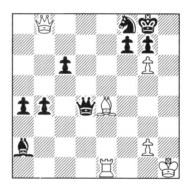

In a position which was already good for Black, White has just blundered with 40 g5-g6?. Black could have won at once with 40...f5!. If the bishop moves, Black's queen will fork rook and king on h4, which wins immediately.

It is my contention that to benefit from any tactical training, learners must be shown how the tactical opportunity came about in the first place. So including the opening moves is helpful as it gives learners beneficial chess knowledge that a certain tactical opportunity can arise from a certain opening with a certain pawn structure. The tactical skill must be developed only this way for the learner to beneficially accrue practical gains in this area of chess knowledge. With this knowledge, the learner will be able to play towards a tactical situation or choose moves in an opening or middlegame that will give rise to a tactical motif. I do not argue that the learner disregards the tedious learning of basic tactical motifs by name. In fact mastery of the basics is a mandatory requirement for any further study. There shouldn't be any doubt in your mind what a double attack or a skewer or a pin looks like.

In one of my few lectures, I carried out exercises where I showed students some puzzles lacking in specifics. Some students would try to solve the puzzle from the viewpoint of the losing side, of course, not knowing who possesses the tactical opportunity. Some students could not recognize the opening from which the pawn structure arose. One must be reminded that a chess game entails the playing of the opening and sometimes the middlegame before these opportunities are present on the board. If chess began with a static position plus a hint as to who was winning, and the number of moves it took to deliver the winning blow, then the mainstream approach of learning tactics would make sense. This, however, simply becomes a puzzle-solving contest.

The traditional book is constrained by production costs in packaging its presentation of chess knowledge. In the interest of saving costs, it presents the puzzle to the solver at the point where the tactical sequence begins. This particular way of learning tactics benefits mostly the advanced players, since they already possess the knowledge with regards to the source opening by simply noting the pawn structure. The tactical motif or picture becomes a knowledge entity where it is saved in the brain under a meaningful category for easy recall in over-the-board use. This is why advanced players will intuitively choose moves that channel the game to a recognized position where one or a number of tactical motifs fit.

For example, the well-known bishop sacrifice on h7 is usually something an experienced player will intuitively recognize as effective if there is a pawn or a piece on e5 controlling f6. A most recent example from my experience occurred in the first round of the US Open this year against a young standout rated 2276 USCF.

Game 11
A.Hortillosa-D.Studen
US Open, Indianapolis 2009
Scandinavian Defence

1 e4 d5 2 exd5 ♕xd5 3 ♘c3 ♕a5 4 ♘f3 ♘f6 5 d4 c6 6 ♗c4 ♗g4 7 h3 ♗xf3 8 ♕xf3 e6 9 0-0 ♗e7 10 ♗f4 ♘bd7 11

♖fe1 ♘b6 12 ♗d3 ♘bd5 13 ♘xd5 cxd5 14 c3 0-0 15 ♗e5 b5 16 a3 ♕b6 17 ♖e3 a5 18 ♕e2 b4 19 cxb4 axb4 20 a4 ♘d7

After my last move, both sides have equal chances to play for a win. But his unexpected response right away felt just wrong and looked very suspicious. I thought for a long time working out the details of the combination to its conclusion and after fact-checking it twice I struck with:

21 ♗xh7+ ♔xh7 22 ♕h5+ ♔g8 23 ♗xg7

None of these ideas are original yet these double-bishop sacrifices are fun to make on the board.

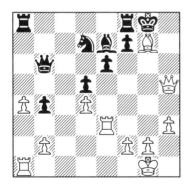

23...f5

He could try 23...♔xg7 but this would lead to mate as well after 24 ♖g3+ ♔f6 25 ♕g5.

24 ♖g3 ♗h4

One last attempt to delay the inevitable.

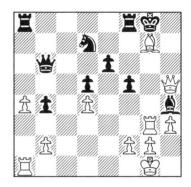

25 ♗f6+ 1-0

25...♗xg3 26 ♕g6 is mate

Another example would be some recognition that an advanced f-pawn allows a rook lift f1-f3-g3 or h3. When the position warrants this conduct of an attack, one must then avoid moving the g- or h-pawn as it will only impede the transfer of the rook to either file. A further example is the motif where there is a white pawn on g6 and the White player sacrifices a rook on h8 to be followed by a queen check on the h-file which can result in a mate on h7, assuming of course that the f8-square is occupied, and the h-file is open.

In my proposed approach, the reader also learns how the conditions for a tactical blow come about. Against strong players, these opportunities do not just appear by chance. Master players of the game in practice would laboriously manoeuvre their pieces to arrive at their respective striking points for which a tactical combination is possible. Just knowing the markers on the path will help us tremendously in getting there.

I hear amateurs lament to this effect when playing over grandmaster games, "*If I can just get to this position, I will beat this grandmaster too.*" Does it sound familiar? We hear ourselves say this all the time, in the sound of a wish. And if only we can get ourselves to these "White to move and win in 5" positions, our brain can be easily primed and prodded to look for the winning tactical sequence. Only then can we outplay a master player and proudly share kinship with one.

In summary, it is vital that we make a distinction between the study of tactics and the sharpening of our tactical abilities. The former involves and limits its interests to knowing tactical concepts, recognizing tactical motifs and understanding the structural conditions of their occurrence. The latter strictly limits its sphere to the actual solving of tactical puzzles or doing tactical exercises. The former uses primarily reading or coaching as the principal linkage of acquiring knowledge. The latter focuses exclusively on activities involving the actual routine of solving puzzles either using a tactics server, software like Convecta's CT-ART 3, a tactical book or a combination of these.

Are Openings Really Important?

The number of books and articles written on opening theory indeed abounds. Our appetite for this genre is insatiable. Our wanton indulgence, it seems, leaves us gorging on the wrong kind of food. Just like the fat in one's diet, it tastes good but is downright harmful. The benefit is temporary but the damage is lasting. We consume it far more than we do equally important facets of the game like tactics, middlegame strategy and endgame techniques. The lack of variety leads to lingering indigestion.

One only has to examine his or her own library to find corroborating proof to this assertion. I, myself, have irrationally spent large sums of money years back hoarding books on openings I do not even play. I guess I bought them because I wanted to learn these openings and make them part of my repertoire. Many are collecting dust, not deserving even a casual perusal. For that matter, I have books I have yet to read from cover to cover. Our quick victories in the opening give rise to our misplaced devotion to opening novelties and their dedicated study as a way to attain sustainable growth in chess. Haven't we heard the sage declaration that all openings are playable below master level?

Since we mentioned opening study in passing and our irrational obsession for its mastery, allow me this opportunity to digress as the following important points need reinforcing. This rapidplay encounter between two grandmasters started as a standard Sicilian Defence until move five:

Game 12
H.Stefansson-J.Arnason
Kopavogur (rapid) 2000
Sicilian Defence

1 e4 c5 2 ♘f3 ♘c6 3 d4 cxd4 4 ♘xd4 ♕c7 5 ♘c3 a6?!

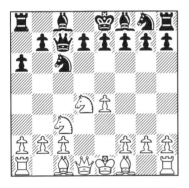

5...e6 will reach a Taimanov, but what is this? Did the faster tempo of the game cause Black to mix up the lines? Here we see that even grandmasters, for whatever reason, can sometimes slip up and confuse their lines.

6 ♘d5 ♕d8 7 ♗e3 ♖b8

This move anticipates White exchanging knights on c6, when after ...bxc6 the rook will have an open file simultaneously attacking b2 and defending against ♗b6. White for sure took time to understand the motiva-

tion behind Black's somewhat unusual move order. Rather than willingly cooperating with Black in the peaceful exchange of knights on c6, he found a more sinister response with this shocker:

8 ♘b5! axb5 9 ♗b6

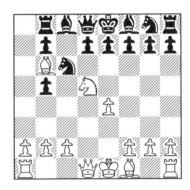

White wins the queen, and ultimately the game.

This is a learning example of one reacting correctly to something unfamiliar. When your opponent plays a move disrespected by the theoretical body in a rather familiar opening, wisely pause and search for what is wrong with it. While not all non-book moves are necessarily bad, there are usually good reasons why they are infrequent in master practice. If you cannot find anything wrong, then proceed normally as you would with established lines.

The other side of this point is: Should you avoid lines not well regarded by theory? Do we build a structure on top of an unsteady foundation? Of course we don't because we respect a body of theory governing the strength of materials. Challenge this body of theory, which has stood the test of time, irresponsibly and you will find yourself in the middle of suffocating rubbles. In general, strong players are quick to notice the inaccuracy and are more precise in the just dispense of its punishment. Because these inaccuracies occur frequently in our play, we conclude it is best mitigated by studying more openings. The simplest and most effective fix for amateurs is to limit our opening repertoire to main lines employed by grandmasters.

Opening play is one aspect of chess study in which the plagiarizing of grandmaster ideas has become not only practically necessary but deemed highly laudable. I am not categorically opposed to the championing of sidelines; I am merely advocating prudence in its use. In my opinion, creative experimentation finds its proper place only in master level chess. The fastest route to master level chess is not by innovating but by emulating with understanding. For this reason we are implored to invest in the study of master games.

It is baffling to see why amateurs are so drawn to sidelines. I guess it is the prospect of a quick win that attracts us to these dubious lines. There is illogic in the thinking that sidelines will give us better chances of outplaying stronger opponents. I submit to you that the truth lies on the far and opposite side. Stronger players are better in

confusing us with sidelines than we are at confusing them. I also suspect stronger players actually wince inside when weaker players confidently choose the main lines. Because then it would mean long and arduous work on their part to score the win. For sure, the win for the stronger side will seldom come prematurely in the opening.

I often hear weaker players say, "I do not like book lines because then I have to study a lot and it's just too hard." This attitude is encouraged by well-meaning chess coaches when they advise their wards to not study openings too much. In truth, the problem is attributable to unclear messages and our tendency to only hear what we want to hear. This happens a lot when this development quirk which served us well during our childhood years continues unchecked into adulthood. What coaches really care about is less study of openings and more study of other chess essentials, but often students hear the pleading to mean too much opening study is unhealthy and lacks utility. The hard truth about opening study is that it is essential; it is hard, and it is unavoidable. But it can be made "easy" hard by informed copying.

When you hear anyone say to you that what you need in the opening is a good understanding of general opening principles and nothing more to play the game – your best move here is to ignore their pretentious advice. Any understanding of general opening principles short of knowing some book lines is futile because it only works when your opponent is following the same dictum. More often, the breathing person on the other side of the board knows more than just general principles. Chess is a concrete game and you have to think moves in a very concrete way if you care to do well. Gone are the days when knowing general opening principles and feel for development are enough to get you to a playable middlegame. Those days were the romantic years of chess just before the pre-computer and pre-Internet days. The sooner you wake up to this paradigm shift, the faster you get to your desired improvement goal in chess.

The problem chess coaches rant against is not the superficiality of book knowledge but book knowledge without understanding. The one who understands the difference reaps the most benefit. We cannot condemn one side of the coin to extol the virtues of the other side. When we do, we render the coin unacceptable as legal tender; therefore, it becomes useless. The memorization of many sharp lines in some openings is nothing short of necessary. But when memorization is emphasized at the expense of proper understanding our creative experience suffers. Then our play becomes very mechanical and it robs chess of the joys we proclaim to pursue. We are attracted to chess because the mere play-

ing allows us to discover and explore the hidden artistry in us. It is the understanding that enlivens one's body of chess knowledge, but it is their blended effort that is capable of producing great artefacts of struggles etched in chess scores to be admired and played many times over by masters and amateurs alike everywhere.

One example of reckless exuberance placed on rote memorization of opening lines from my own experience was my game against FM Michael Langer, who qualified and played in two US Chess Championships in 2007 and 2008.

Game 13
M.Langer-A.Hortillosa
San Antonio 2001
Sicilian Defence

1 e4 c5 2 ♘f3 ♘c6 3 d4 cxd4 4 ♘xd4 g6 5 c4 ♗g7 6 ♗e3 ♘f6 7 ♘c3 ♘g4

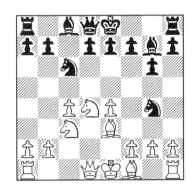

I was drawn to 8...♘g4 primarily because the three popular books on the Accelerated Dragon in my growing chess library have pointed out numerous instances in which White players have fallen victim to this tricky sideline. My attraction to it is reinforced by the frequency of these dramatic downfalls, the ease by which these downfalls are staged and the fairly strong calibre of its victims. In these examples, the many wins by Black came about directly as a result of White players merely playing natural-looking moves. From the diagrammed position, if White continues simply following general opening principles as a guide, he often ends up caught in an inferior line. It seems true that sometimes you simply must know certain theory to avoid this happening.

The first opportunity for White to go wrong is with this inaccurate queen-exchange manoeuvre starting with 8 ♘xc6. Many games continue with 8...♘xe3 9 ♘xd8 ♘xd1 10 ♖xd1, but enlightened White players who know some theory prefer to recapture with 10 ♘xd1 which is considered to be more precise by most opening experts.

What puts the capture on d1 with a rook instead of the knight under a cloud is the move 10...♗xc3+. Unless you know the theory this in-between move will escape the mind of most players below master level for various reasons, but foremost is our bias towards the idea of preferring a bishop for a knight. Also, the idea of exchanging the dark-squared bishop in Black's chosen set-up, even for its counterpart,

is generally thought to be bad.

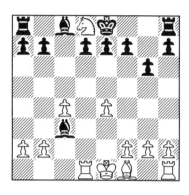

Here is another case of concrete reasoning based on concrete moves trumping general principles. The parting of the bishop will not compromise Black's weakened dark squares on the kingside because in the absence of White's queen and dark-squared bishop, the weak squares there cannot be profitably exploited. Meanwhile, the recapture on c3 fractures White's queenside pawns. The endgame is known to be favourable to Black after 11 bxc3 ♔xd8.

The actual game continued:

8 ♕xg4 ♘xd4 9 ♕d1 e5

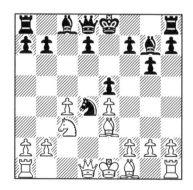

Laying the initial phase of a trap. This is another juncture where White players get tripped up, especially the pawn snatchers.

10 ♘b5

This move is a possible signal that White is oblivious to the trap. During the game I wondered whether Langer was aware of the looming danger if White is not careful with his next move. But first I had to complete the final phase of the trap.

10...0-0 11 ♘xd4

The exchange on d4 gives White the option to win a pawn if he so desires. Will he?

11...exd4 12 ♗xd4

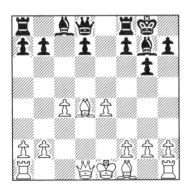

Yes, he did win a pawn, but at what cost? Before continuing on, compare the pawn structures, material count, development and piece quality of both camps and see if you can make a judgment as to which side is better. What is Black's threat?

12...♕a5+

It was noticeable that this move came as a shock. What happened here

is that we were both proven wrong in our expectations by our assumptions. My opponent assumed that I had carelessly blundered a pawn. I did not expect his ignorance of the line given his high rating and obvious tournament experience. To be fair, it is also possible he simply had forgotten.

As it turns out White has no acceptable way of parrying the check so his king is forced to take a walk and give up castling privileges.

13 ♔e2 ♖e8

The threat against e4 increases Black's lead in development.

14 f3 d5

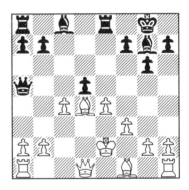

I am sure you are not thinking that I came up with this sequence at the board, are you? This is all book knowledge. Up to this point, I just had to remember the sequence impeccably as laid out in the books. I tried hard to postpone any celebratory tendencies, but a smile broke out prematurely. It is indeed a challenge hiding your glee after catching a very strong player in an opening trap.

15 ♗xg7 ♖xe4+

White cannot take the rook on e4 because of 16...♗g4+ winning the queen. But his next move threw me off.

16 ♔d3

Here is a case where one side, the stronger player, was thinking and sweating out to survive the harsh realities of his present predicament. In contrast, you have the weaker player trying to win with the least effort by relying mostly on what he had seen in books and ignoring concrete lines duly vetted by hard calculations.

I expected 16 ♔f2 ♕c5+ 17 ♔g3 ♕e3 18 h3 ♕f4+ 19 ♔f2 ♗xg7, as seen in the books, with Black having the advantage.

16...♖xc4 17 ♔e3

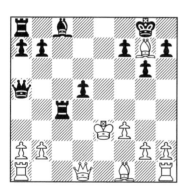

White's defiant dance got me confused and quickly led to the following error:

17...♔xg7?

The correct way to continue is with 17...♕c5+. Here 18 ♗d4 would not suffice because of 18...♕e7+ when 19 ♔f2 ♕h4+ 20 g3 ♕xd4+ 21 ♕xd4 ♖xd4 has

Black emerging a pawn up.

18 ♗xc4

After this obvious capture on c4, Black is left down an exchange and I resigned shortly.

Count this as fair warning for those who labour exceedingly hard on their array of traps. Catching the unwary in your web does not guarantee easy feeding after all. Long hours wasted on memorizing repertoire lines so chosen because of their crafty underpinnings are better spent on honing your calculation skills. Being familiar with these traps does not harm. It is the sole reliance on traps as trusted means to achieve short wins that is to be avoided. To the prey who finds himself caught in the web – never surrender. The books sing of heroes who have survived the cleverest traps. Do not yield without a fight. Resolve to mount the stiffest resistance. Dampen his gloat with the most discomfort you can muster on the board.

In the next part of this chapter, we will consider the details of my chess thinking process as an enabler in diminishing blunders and spotting tactical opportunities. The terms chess thinking process and system are used interchangeably throughout the book.

Types of Errors in Chess

For the sake of framing our discussion in the proper context, let's classify errors by the magnitude of their impact on the outcome of the game. But first note that the word "blunder" by definition is a gross error. In most cases, as our experience attests, one blunder is enough to decide a game. However, some moves, which cannot be classified as blunders by our definition, should be labelled as errors because at the time they were played, better alternatives existed.

The playing of an inferior move in our construct is an error just the same. These particular errors are survivable as single events and have lesser impact on the final outcome of the game. If not corrected, however, the cumulative effects of these errors can be fatal. In practice, it is only the presence of a large advantage that keeps a win or a draw uncompromised despite the error. We want to eliminate even this type of error because we aim for near perfection. As a practical matter, continually missing opportunities can be a big letdown leading to dire consequences. We will put a spotlight on these error types when we consider how the system can be used to spot tactical opportunities and exploit combination motifs due to errors by our opponents.

In our quest for chess improvement, failing to exploit a winning opportunity is equally to be avoided as playing a blunder. It is not enough to simply prevent our own blunders, because winning requires obviously much more. We have to be just as alert in exploiting weaknesses and blunders of the opposing side. Both abilities must be honed to attain the desired lasting chess improvement. A bad move becomes a bona fide blunder only if the other side notices the error and exploits it to his advantage.

A recent example of a missed opportunity is my first-round game against IM David Pruess at the 2009 Copper State Invitational. No one likes a player who hides behind excuses but first-round games are unique in the sense that they tend to influence our demeanour for the rest of the tournament.

Game 14
D.Pruess-A.Hortillosa
Copper State Invitational,
Mesa 2009
Sicilian Defence

1 e4 c5 2 ♘f3 g6 3 d4 cxd4 4 ♘xd4 ♗g7 5 ♘c3 ♘c6 6 ♗e3 ♘f6 7 ♗c4 ♕a5 8 0-0 0-0 9 ♘b3 ♕c7 10 ♗e2 a6 11 f4 d6 12 g4 e6 13 ♕e1 b5 14 g5 ♘e8 15 ♖d1 ♘e7 16 ♗d3 ♗b7 17 ♕h4 f5 18 gxf6 ♗xf6 19 ♕g4 ♘g7 20 ♘d4

IM Pruess is known for his attacking prowess and aggressive play. He already has two GM norms and it is just a matter of time before he earns the last one. This being the first round and my first encounter with the 9 ♘b3 line, I thought I would either get clobbered early or later. Reaching move ten, I thought I had fallen into a bad opening line. I was so impressed by White's opening scheme because he looked so far ahead in development. However, my real downfall in this game was not my ignorance of this line but rather it was my overly cautious approach. I played the opponent and not the board.

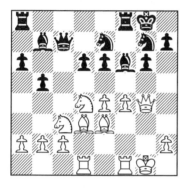

Had I been playing a lesser chess god, I would have spent precious clock time checking out the falsity of his last move. Sadly, I spent all my thinking time looking for a viable defence to his threat on e6. Instead of nullifying his threat with a bigger threat, I fearfully acquiesced to his; in doing so I missed the opportunity of exploiting his blunder. I did not see it primarily because I did not even care to look. In this game, I skipped steps two and three of my system because I trusted the judgment of my strong opponent.

The strong counter in 20...♕b6 refutes White's idea:

a) The 21 ♘f5 try loses immediately because of 21...exf5 22 ♗xb6 fxg4 winning a piece.

b) White's best chance is 21 e5. Play

might continue 21...dxe5 22 fxe5 ♗xe5 23 ♖xf8+ ♖xf8 24 ♗e4 ♗xe4 25 ♕xe4 ♕c7 with advantage to Black.

In the game I replied with the silly 20...♗c8. A move later, I blundered and lost the game shortly thereafter. We both saw that the move was a blunder the moment it was executed. Unfortunately, IM Pruess proved more alert than me in punishing the inaccuracies.

The System – An Introduction

How do we prevent these errors from cropping up? Can we really effectively diminish the occurrence of blunders in our games? The answer is a resounding yes! The solution I propose is a formalized system of chess thinking. This system is claimed to be formalized because the practitioner is disallowed to vary from the process steps. It is described as a process because it is limited to a series of steps which are sequential in order. Skipping a step is dangerous and renders the system devoid of its intrinsic distinction as a process. In other words, all the steps must be observed and followed at all times in all conditions during play, at least during the assimilation period.

By the way, regardless of varying chess abilities, we all employ some kind of chess thinking before arriving at the chosen move. Some of us have a good and consistent move selection algorithm mirroring the kind employed in chess programming. The avowed system shares the same robust characteristics. For those who are looking for a reliable system, this is a boon to you.

For the system to be effective, one must apply it consistently without digression, at every turn to move, in all phases of the game from the opening to middlegame and endgame. One has to only note that it takes just one of these types of errors to tilt the balance of the contest to a consequential result. Consistency, which means uniform application of the system for the entire duration of the game, is the key. Do not fault the system if it delivers inconsistent results for you because of laziness and failure to consistently apply it to your play. Only strict compliance augurs promising results.

The System – A Brief Description

What sorts of "thinking actions" are involved in this process? The easiest way to explain this notion is by way of game fragments as in the examples, below. But first, let's outline the steps:

1. Initiate a broad reconnaissance of the position to gather key data elements

Key questions: Which piece or pieces are undefended? Which squares are weak? Is my king position safe? Is the opponent's king safer than mine? Which piece is undeveloped? Which piece needs repositioning? Which piece is lacking escape squares if threatened? What Silman imbalances exist on the board? On which section of the board do I enjoy a preponderance of mate-

rial? For a better understanding of imbalances as catalogued by IM Silman, consult his best-selling book *How To Reassess Your Chess*.

2. Search for specific threats

Key questions: What are the opponent's immediate or latent threats? What, if anything, does his last move threaten?

3. Rank the severity of the threats

Key questions: Is the threat real or valid? If the threat is real, can I ignore it? Can I nullify the threat by creating or executing my own threat?

4. Focus your response against the threat with the highest degree of harm if ignored or not prevented

Key question: Which threat is the most harmful if not prevented?

5. Search for candidate moves

Key questions: Which candidate move best responds to the threat? Does this move, if executed, create or execute even more serious threats?

6. Execute the move in your head

Key questions: How does the move alter the position on the board? Does the piece chosen to move currently perform a vital function? What happens if the function is no longer performed as a result of the move? What structural changes on the board occurred because of the move?

7. Conduct a post-reconnaissance of the position after the chosen candidate move is mentally executed

8. If reconnaissance yields a bigger harm as a result of the move, repeat steps 5 to 7 until a safe or correct move is derived

Over time, the process steps become abbreviated in their execution details as you gain mastery of the entire sequence. As you improve, you will know when to shorten or even skip a step, but for now try to consistently apply the process in its entirety. Your own results will tell you when you can begin varying from the sequence or even deleting or adding a step.

Remember that your primary concern ought to be the reduction or near elimination of game-ending blunders. I say that because the same system can be used in finding game-winning tactical combinations for you. As you get stronger, you will develop a general system approach where you combine this system with other general planning and strategic principles which will cogently guide your entire thinking during the prosecution of the entire game. When that day arrives, you will no longer need this book. It will be a happy day for both of us.

Other Relevant Tactics Theory

Elemental to chess improvement is a background understanding of some things in chess theory. So, the following is a necessary digression and a repetition of some concepts discussed above. This is by design. I want us to preface every juncture in the discussion, if possible, with old knowledge thereby reinforcing our understanding of the key parts while cementing our overall grasp of the subject matter as a whole.

There are two types of errors: namely, errors of omission and errors of commission. Examples of the former occur when we fail to notice a tactical opportunity leading to a huge advantage on the board. A somewhat common variety of this error involves choosing a move resulting in a slower win rather than a much quicker one. For the sake of chess perfection, the error, while still winning, can be termed a minor error of omission. Errors of omission are simply the types that fail to execute the best move from among the available legal options.

The primary focus of the system is to address the latter type of error which I call errors of commission. These are the errors we commit on the board brought about by gross oversights, chess blindness and miscalculations. This genre of errors is almost always tactical in nature and decisive in outcome. The usual result of these errors is material loss.

When It's Okay Not to Use the System

Obviously we can skip the application

of the system in the early moves of the opening as contact is usually minimal during this phase for most openings. However, there are certain openings requiring the application of the system as early as move three.

The system has some implicit assumptions. One such assumption is knowing when to invoke the system. If you are certain that you are playing book lines, then you can save time by skipping the system. As soon as contact between pawns or pieces is initiated or the divide in territory is crossed, it is prudent to invoke the system at once. *Your success is correlated to the level of diligence in your application of the system.*

Be alert to invoke the system when the opponent makes a long move outside the safe confines of his territorial control, like ...♛a5 in the next example. Over time, you will develop a feel for when to invoke the system. This happens when you achieve some degree of efficiency in its use. One other situation to watch out for is when you observe a move not so well regarded by theory. Again, there are concrete reasons why some opening moves are not included as theory.

While the system can be and should be applied in all phases of the game, it is only the timing or the "when" to invoke the system that varies. Our first example invokes the system in the opening phase of the game. By the way, the process steps must be verbalized in

the head. Hearing your mind talk clarifies the steps, cements options and ensures none of the steps are skipped.

The System in Action – Example 1

Let's follow a game where Black chooses the venerable Cambridge Springs Defence against the Queen's Gambit. Only six moves into the game, White finds himself already at a critical juncture:

1 d4 d5 2 c4 e6 3 ♘c3 ♘f6 4 ♗g5 ♘bd7 5 e3 c6 6 ♘f3 ♛a5

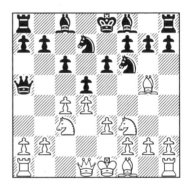

When I say critical, I mean White is already presented with options requiring apt decisions. Options on the board, as we said earlier, mean opportunities for errors.

Step 1: Initiate a broad reconnaissance of the position

One will observe that both players, up to this point, have followed sound book lines. Black's last move defines the Cambridge Springs Defence. There is contact between the c4-pawn and the d5-pawn. The black knight on f6 is attacked by the bishop on g5. The bishop on g5 is supported by the knight on f3. Curiously, the black queen has just left its original square; a move generally frowned upon by opening theorists in most circumstances but not in the Cambridge Springs. The queen on a5 pins the knight on c3 thereby hampering its mobility.

Step 2: Search for specific threats

What are *all* the threats? What is the previous move threatening or attacking? Which threat is immediate? Which ones are latent or covert?

With the move 6...♛a5, what is the queen threatening or attacking? The answer is usually long and descriptive like so: "The queen on a5 attacks along its path directly and indirectly, the knight on c3, the king on e1, the pawn on a2, the rook on a1, and the bishop on g5." In some cases, the attacked elements are not just pieces but include the squares along the path of influence. While it is true that some of the pieces on the path of influence are only indirectly attacked, there are variations where even these pieces are in danger of capture. Keeping that thought in mind during play will save you some headaches.

Never examine candidate moves until the threat search is completed. It is simply a waste of time. *Most blunders occur when threats are not actively sought and responded to adequately.* Often, they are not found because there was no active search in the first place. *Chess Cafe* columnist Dan Heisman, in his popular Internet Chess Club lectures, suggests adding the word "*all*" as it suggests to the mind the expansive nature of the search.

Step 3: Rank the severity of the threats

Is the threat real or valid? If the threat is real, can I ignore it? Can I nullify the threat by my own threat? Can I ignore the threat?

If the threat is against the king, you must momentarily pause your own activity and mitigate against this threat first. Threats against the king are fatal. In this instance the threat is not against the king, but directly against the knight on c3 and indirectly against the bishop on g5. Can I counter with a bigger threat? You look for undefended pieces. You look for overloaded pieces. (Overloaded pieces are pieces fulfilling multiple functions such as defending another piece, defending a pawn or pawns, and defending a key square.) You look for pieces with limited escape squares. You look for pieces which are on the same colour square. These pieces are vulnerable to forks and skewers. White has no threat of his own and, therefore, cannot counter with a bigger threat. Since White has no counter threat, and he cannot ignore the threat, he proceeds to step four.

Step 4: Focus your response against the threat with the highest degree of harm if ignored or not prevented

Seeing the threats, White will recognize that the knight on c3, if attacked by another piece, will lead to the loss of a pawn if left undefended. Since the knight is pinned to the king, the square it occupies, in a sense, is also under attack. The obvious pieces that can establish contact in one move with the square is the black knight on f6 and the bishop on f8. Knowing this, White should consider preventing the knight from reaching the attacking entry point, which is e4. The threat against the knight on c3 is real and cannot be ignored. While ...♗b4 is also a threat that can be established in one move, ...♘e4 is the most obvious threat requiring immediate attention as it also attacks g5. You may consider the ...♗b4 threat a latent one.

Step 5: Search for candidate moves

Which candidate move best responds to the threat? Does this move if executed create even more serious threats? Some responses leave behind trailing threats. Start with the moves that protect against the direct threat, which is against the knight on c3. One way of protecting the knight is to stop another hostile piece from directly attacking it. In this example, the obvious piece is the knight on f6 landing on e4. A natural choice for White is to defend the e4-square with a bishop by 7 ♗d3.

The simple idea is to capture the knight landing on e4 with the bishop (7...♘e4 8 ♗xe4 dxe4). This looks logical as it develops a piece and prepares castling. But we cannot know yet for sure if indeed this is the right move until the rest of the steps are carried out.

Step 6: Execute the move in your head

How does the move alter the position on the board? Does the piece chosen to move currently perform a vital function? What happens if the function is no longer performed as a result of the move? What structural changes on the board would occur because of the move? This helps in seeing what happens when a move is chosen and executed. Imagine the move played on the board. This may be difficult at first but it becomes easier over time. Force yourself into doing this each time. After playing out our intended line 7 ♗d3 ♘e4 8 ♗xe4 dxe4 in our head, we clearly fix the resulting position in our mind as we proceed to the next step.

Step 7: Conduct a post-reconnaissance of the position after the chosen candidate move is mentally executed

Most times, after seeing the candidate move executed and the resulting position clearly formed in our mind, we immediately see the error. How often do we see our own blunder just as we have touched the piece? Why did we not see the blunder while reflecting on the move as a candidate? My guess is that the move is really never fixed in our mind until it is executed even though we saw the move as a candidate. We see but we are not seeing. I think the mystery is explained as a biological function more than a physical inability. It is the same function which helps us not fear our imagination because our minds by design place a strong distinction between the imagined and the real. It seems that the brain is unable or better yet unwilling to see the dangers of the imagined until it becomes real. So the idea is to trick the brain to see the imagined being made real by actually fixing the image in our mind's eye.

Another plausible explanation is using the analogy of taking a picture of a scene. The scene is there but we are not really "seeing" the details until we have snapped the picture. Picturing the move as executed on the board is not the same as merely seeing the move as a candidate. There is a huge difference in effort.

At other times, the error is not seen until the intended follow-up is played out. This is because some errors are not embodied in single moves but in pairs with the second move as part of a single idea. In this instance the candidate move forms the head of the blunder and the second move, which is consequentially harmful as the tail.

Always consider the structural changes that occur after the move is executed, especially with pawn moves.

A vacated square is open for occupation by hostile pieces. It can serve as a jumping point into your territory. The simple advance of a pawn may sometimes unblock a diagonal, a file or a rank exposing other pieces to threats of capture.

If one examines the resulting structural changes after the recapture by Black on e4 with the pawn, it will be noticed that the knight on f3 is now attacked by the recapturing pawn. The other change that is hard to notice without purposeful examination is that the queen on a5 now directly attacks the bishop on g5 because the pawn on d5 that used to block the queen's attack path has moved to e4. If White plays the careless 9 ♘fd2, which is the real blunder, he loses the bishop on g5. White will be forced to play 9 ♘e5 avoiding the loss of a piece but also giving Black a fine game. Most White players will not concede the advantage of the first move in this manner and so will conclude that a better move should be chosen other than 7 ♗d3 on the grounds that the intended follow-up will not suffice as adequate response to the threat.

Step 8: If reconnaissance yields a bigger harm as a result of the move, repeat steps 5, 6 and 7 until a safe or correct move is derived

Since the proposed response against the threat does not "adequately" prevent the intrusion of the knight on e4, and because capturing the knight with the bishop on d3 is a weak follow-up, we dismiss ♗d3 as a suitable candidate. The system helped us foresee a potential blunder and helped us realize the insufficiency of our candidate move. So, we return to step five for the next iteration until we find an adequate response.

The second look for candidate moves yields 7 ♘d2 as a plausible choice. This move protects the e4 square and unpins the other knight on c3. If Black continues with 7...♘e4, White will simply capture with 8 ♘dxe4. When Black recaptures with the pawn on d5, the pawn is no longer attacking anything on f3. White can then use the tempo to move the bishop away from the queen's attack. A knight has been exchanged for a knight, an even trade. Meanwhile, the Black pawn on e4 is overextended and will need protection. Black's control of d5 is also diminished, which can be detrimental to him in some lines.

Our second choice will adequately defuse the threat so our search for the best candidate is finally derived. Diligently follow the steps in the specified order until they all cohere in a game from start to finish as your clock situation will allow.

The System in Action – Example 2 (Abbreviated Version)

Here's a clash between two giants at the 2006 Tal Memorial:

Game 15
L.Aronian-P.Svidler
Tal Memorial, Moscow 2006
Grünfeld Defence

1 d4 ♘f6 2 c4 g6 3 ♘c3 d5 4 ♗g5 ♘e4 5 ♗h4 ♘xc3 6 bxc3 dxc4 7 e3 ♗e6 8 ♕b1 ♕d5 9 ♘f3 ♘d7 10 ♗e2 ♗f5 11 ♕b2 ♗g7 12 0-0 ♘b6 13 a4 a5 14 ♘d2 ♗d3 15 ♗xd3 cxd3 16 ♖fb1 ♕c6 17 ♕a3 0-0 18 c4 ♘xc4 19 ♘xc4 ♕xc4 20 ♗xe7 ♖fe8 21 ♖d1 ♖ac8 22 ♗g5 c5 23 ♕xd3

White's last move attacks the black queen on c4 and offers the exchange of queens. You can rightly assume that both players are constantly doing a general reconnaissance of the position before and after every move. Svidler saw the immediate threat to his queen but correctly delayed the exchange of queens and captured on d4 with the c-pawn, enabling the support of his queen with his rook on c8:

23...cxd4

By playing this move, Black saddles White with the responsibility of making a choice from a few reasonable-looking options. We know options can be a catalyst for error because the possessor of options is forced to calculate the consequences for each candidate option. This is unlike forcing lines, where your choice is usually limited to one – for ill or for good, you have to make the move.

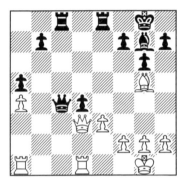

Let us now take the White side and employ the system to decide our next move. Let us assume that we have been continually updating our reconnaissance data. We know the general terrain. We see that presently Black is ahead by a pawn. So we have to figure out a way to restore the material balance. We are aware of all the contact points. We are also aware that the black bishop on g7 is indirectly attacking the rook on a1 and so forth.

Do we have a forcing reply that will give us an advantage? The answer is no. Taking the queen first on c4 is a forcing reply, but it will only bring another heavy piece to c4 attacking d4. Let us not straight away dismiss this

reply because it is not clear upon cursory examination if that really matters.

If you are following carefully, we are now on step three. We now continue to the next step and search for all threats mentally noting the degree of harm of each threat if left ignored or not prevented. Do we have a threat that nullifies Black's threat? The answer again is no. Can we ignore his threat or threats? The answer once more is no.

Now, we search for candidate replies starting with the biggest threat. Let us say that the biggest threat is the threat against the pawn on e3 and then the rook on a1, which will be exposed to capture by the black bishop after ...dxe3.

Let's look at the reply 24 e3xd4. First, what structural change did the move create in our position. Answer: The file is now open and only one rook is controlling the file – not White's but Black's. The pawn on d4 is now White's not Black's. The threat to the rook on a1 is practically eliminated because it is presently blocked by the pawn. So far these are the obvious changes to the position. One other observation that is of concern to us is that the material balance is for now restored.

If we are alert, we will notice that the enemy rook controlling the open file now has access to our back rank and can give check to the white king. Well, we already know that all checks must be attended to. The rules of chess force us to first parry the check by any means before making another legal move. It is akin to losing a turn at bat.

After a careful examination, we will find that a check on e1 can only be parried by capturing the checking piece with our own. The only piece that can legally do it is the rook on d1. Here, we finally see the real danger: the rook on d1 performs a crucial defensive role supporting the queen on d3. This tactic is called deflection or overloading a function. Suddenly, White's rook on d1 is forced to perform two functions: the defence of the queen on d3 and the defence against a check on the king. Black forcibly deflects the rook on d1 from the defence of the queen on d3. We now see that the recapture 24 e3xd4 is a gross blunder. We successfully avoided it and now we continue to search for other candidate replies with least or no harm.

In the actual game even a world-class player like Aronian blundered with **24 exd4??**. Svidler got to play **24...♖e1+!** and White resigned.

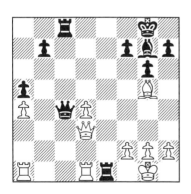

We limited our employment of the system to preventing errors of commission in our last example. The system is effectual as well in preventing errors of omission. We will not repeat the exercise to see how that works because essentially the process steps are exactly the same.

It must be noted, however, that errors of omission are usually survivable whereas errors of commission are generally fatal. Therefore, more care has to be given to its handling, and preventing such errors should be our biggest concern in the first order. If we can just eliminate these errors, quick and ego-bruising defeats will become few and far between. When this is finally achieved in your game, the jousting experience becomes satisfying and rewarding.

Now, let's consider some recent games through the rigors of the chess thinking process as it should be employed after a higher degree of assimilation. As suggested earlier, the system is also effective in reducing errors of omission. Fewer errors of omission means we have become proficient in exploiting errors of the opposing side. It is reasonably thought that skills are acquired and perfected in three phases, namely: crawl, walk and run. The current exercise can be characterized as the "run" phase. In this construct, the process steps may seem to appear elastic rather than rigid as suggested during the "crawl" phase shown in the earlier examples.

Game 16
H.Nakamura-J.Friedel
US Championship,
Saint Louis 2009
Two Knights Defence

It's the last round of the US Championship, with the prestigious title and $40,000 on the line.

1 e4 e5 2 ♘f3 ♘c6 3 ♗c4 ♘f6 4 ♘g5 d5 5 exd5 ♘a5 6 ♗b5+ c6 7 dxc6 bxc6 8 ♗d3 ♗e7 9 ♘c3 0-0 10 0-0 ♖b8 11 h3 c5 12 b3 ♖b4 13 ♖e1 ♗b7 14 ♗a3 ♖f4 15 g3 ♖d4 16 ♘f3 ♖xd3 17 cxd3 ♕xd3 18 ♘xe5 ♕f5 19 g4 ♕f4

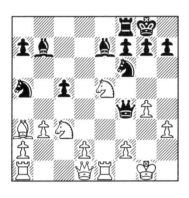

This is a type of position that both players are known to excel at.

20 d4

This move initiates a nasty plan against the black queen.

Reconnaissance: Let's start with Black. He holds the desirable bishop pair and the one on b7 looks ominously dangerous. However, Black cannot easily form a battery to exploit White's airy kingside and weak light squares around

his king. Also, the bishop on e7 is undefended and is therefore susceptible to discovered attacks and his knight on a5 is temporarily out of play. Black has a number of pressing issues which require serious mitigation. He is also an exchange down and against Nakamura or indeed anyone that can be a cause for concern. His rook needs to go to d8 to prevent losing the c5-pawn and he needs to retreat the bishop to a safe square on f8. How about the queen? Just count the safe squares it can go to and you will see a problem. The vulnerability of the black queen is reason enough for White to feel optimistic and for Black to get suspicious.

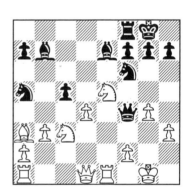

20...♖d8

I am not sure whether Friedel was fully aware that his queen was running out of squares. Perhaps he thought he had time to relocate it to safety. White cannot exploit the queen's lack of squares just yet because if attacked it could take on d4. Meanwhile, pinning the d-pawn and contesting the half-open file seems like a good idea.

On the other hand, one can make a strong argument that Friedel simply did not notice the precarious location of his queen. This could be a case of one operating based on old data. And here's what I meant by that. Black got carried away by the situation on the board and he forgot to refresh his reconnaissance data after White's previous move. With the pawn still sitting on d2, the black queen has access to d4 besides g5 and h6 as safe harbour squares. Another erroneous assumption based on old data is that the bishop on a3 is unable to initiate hostile contact with the queen because the c1-h6 diagonal is still blocked by the d-pawn. Could this possibly be the data set that Friedel was operating on when he chose the rook move? It sounds plausible, but we cannot know for sure.

21 ♕e2

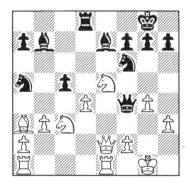

Nakamura feints danger along the d-file so he vacates it, perhaps for the rook on a1. It looks very natural. Then the unthinkable occurs:

21...♖xd4??

Black could try 21...♕h6 gaining time to get off the deadly alley by attacking h3. White would have to abandon his idea to trap the queen and settle for an exchange with 22 ♕e3 to keep his advantage.

22 ♗c1! 1-0

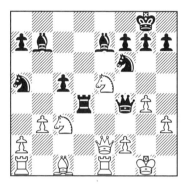

The queen is trapped mid-board. Friedel resigned and Nakamura became the 2009 US Champion.

Let's try some further examples:

> ### Game 17
> **L.Van Wely-J.Sarkar**
> Foxwoods Open,
> Ledyard 2009
> *Grünfeld Defence*

1 d4 ♘f6 2 c4 g6 3 ♘c3 d5 4 cxd5 ♘xd5 5 e4 ♘xc3 6 bxc3 ♗g7 7 ♘f3 c5 8 ♖b1 0-0 9 ♗e2 cxd4 10 cxd4 ♕a5+ 11 ♗d2 ♕xa2 12 0-0 b6 13 ♗g5 ♕e6 14 ♖e1 h6 15 d5 ♕d7 16 ♗f4 ♗a6 17 ♖c1 ♗xe2 18 ♕xe2 a5 19 ♕e3 g5 20 ♗e5 b5 21 ♗xg7 ♔xg7

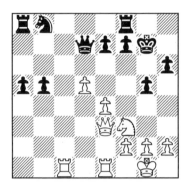

If you were White, how would you continue?

Reconnaissance: Black is a pawn up and his queenside connectors are passed. He is a little behind in development as the knight has not left its original square. If Black catches up in development, his advantage will be clear. White is obligated to strike now while the black knight is still moves away from the defence of the king.

22 ♘xg5

White can play 22 h4 intending 22...gxh4 23 ♘xh4 when the knight invades on f5 leading to a big edge. But the text move is also convincing.

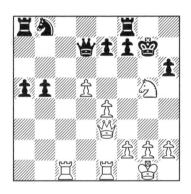

22...hxg5 23 ♕xg5+ ♔h7 24 ♕h5+

This check is important because White wants to check with the rook on g3 instead of h3.

24...♔g7 25 ♖e3 ♖a6

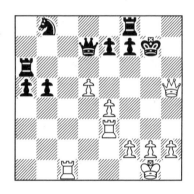

26 ♖c6

What a beautiful interference.

26...♖xc6 27 dxc6 ♕xc6 28 ♖g3+ ♕g6

And White wins the queen. Black resigned after 29 ♕e5+ ♔g8 30 ♖xg6+ fxg6 31 ♕xb5 ♖c8 32 h4 1-0.

Game 18
A.Lenderman-A.Yermolinsky
Foxwoods Open,
Ledyard 2009
King's Indian Defence

1 d4 ♘f6 2 c4 g6 3 ♘c3 ♗g7 4 e4 d6 5 ♘f3 0-0 6 ♗e2 e5 7 0-0 exd4 8 ♘xd4 ♖e8 9 f3 c6 10 ♗f4 ♘h5 11 ♗e3 f5 12 ♕d2 f4 13 ♗f2 ♗e5 14 ♘c2 ♗e6 15 ♘e1 ♘g3 16 ♗xg3 fxg3 17 f4 gxh2+ 18 ♔h1 ♗g7 19 ♖d1 ♘a6 20 f5 ♗f7 21 f6 ♗f8 22 ♘f3 ♘c5 23 ♕f4 a5 24 ♕g3 ♘xe4 25 ♘xe4 ♖xe4 26 ♗d3 ♖e3 27 ♕f4 ♕e8 28 ♕xh2 a4 29 ♘g5 h6 30

♗xg6 ♗xg6 31 f7+ ♗xf7 32 ♘xf7 ♕e6 33 ♕h5 ♖g3

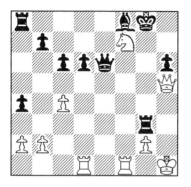

Reconnaissance: White is a pawn down and so he must continue actively. What does Black want with his last move? He wants to play 34...♕g6 offering an exchange of queens and gaining the edge.

Black had a better move than the text with 33...♗g7. Play might continue with 34 ♖xd6 ♕xc4 35 ♘xh6+ ♗xh6 36 ♖g6+ ♗g7 37 ♖xg7+ ♔xg7 38 ♕g5+ ♔h7, and White has nothing better than a perpetual.

How should White exploit Black's inaccuracy?

34 ♖xd6

White's alert response ensures a big advantage. Black overlooked this move probably in time pressure. The brain, conscious of time-saving measures, ignored the move as a possibility because the d6-pawn was defended twice by the bishop and queen. This happens to amateurs more often than to grandmasters. To diminish the frequency of blunders down to a tolerable level in our play, we can never get complacent and must always invest time falsifying every legal option to really establish its impossibility beyond doubt.

The resource only works because it deflects the bishop away from the defence of the sensitive h6-square. I would imagine that it did not take White much time to find it as soon as he understood that in the current position his knight was more valuable and dangerous than his rook on d1. If you have the opportunity to offer an exchange sacrifice to plant a knight in the vicinity of the opposing king, examine it concretely. More often than not the investment will yield better returns. The knight becomes terribly lethal if it combines with the queen.

34...♗xd6 35 ♘xh6+ ♔g7 36 ♘f5+ ♔g8 37 ♘xg3 ♗xg3 38 ♕g5+ ♔h7 39 ♕xg3

Just before reaching the first time control, White regains the sacrificed piece with interest and has a better position.

39...♖e8 40 c5 ♖e7 41 ♕d3+ ♕g6 42 ♖f5

The lack of cover to Black's king invites all kinds of tactical threats. 42 ♖f5 is what I fondly call a hardworking move because it is multi-purpose: it disallows the exchange of queens, disguises a threat to the black queen and protects h5. Tactics always seem to favour the aggressing player with the safer king.

42...♔g7 43 ♕d4+

After this check, Black has only one square to go to without losing big immediately, but even that is losing still.

43...♔g8 44 ♕c4+ ♔g7 45 ♕d4+ ♔g8

46 ♕f4

White could have headed straight

to this position after his 43rd move. Black's resistance finally collapses next move, resulting in the immediate loss of his queen.

46...♕e6 47 ♕g4+ 1-0

> ## Game 19
> ### C.Balogh-P.Drenchev
> Metz 2009
> *Sicilian Defence*

1 e4 c5 2 ♘f3 d6 3 ♘c3 ♘f6 4 d4 cxd4 5 ♕xd4 ♘c6 6 ♗b5 ♗d7 7 ♗xc6 ♗xc6 8 ♗g5 e6 9 0-0-0 ♗e7 10 ♕d3 0-0 11 ♘d4 ♕a5 12 h4 ♖fc8 13 ♔b1 ♖ab8 14 f3 b5 15 g4 b4 16 ♘ce2 ♗a4 17 b3 ♗e8 18 ♗c1 ♖b6 19 ♗b2 d5 20 g5 dxe4 21 fxe4 ♘d7 22 ♘c1 ♘e5 23 ♕e3 ♕c5 24 ♖d2 a5 25 ♘d3 ♘xd3 26 cxd3 ♖bb8 27 ♖c2 ♕d6 28 ♖xc8 ♖xc8 29 ♘f3 ♖d8 30 d4 a4 31 ♘e5 axb3 32 axb3 ♕a6 33 ♖c1 ♖a8 34 ♖c2 f6 35 ♘c4 ♗g6 36 gxf6 ♗xf6 37 ♖h2 ♕c6 38 ♘d2 ♖c8 39 ♕d3

Black's last move created a potent battery along the c-file, seeking to finish White off. White's response was designed to protect the sensitive c2-square from a fatal invasion.

Reconnaissance: Black's powerful bishops are ominously projecting their long-range power into the white camp. White's rook is loose and cannot help in the defence of c2 because a friendly force is blocking its scope of influence. White's knight is tied to the defence of the e4-pawn. Black's b-pawn controls the critical dark squares around the white king. The queen and rook battery is poised to infiltrate along the c-file to decide matters quickly. The only thing that holds up Black's wrath is the queen which also performs another critical function of defending the e-pawn. The b2-bishop also has double duty of protecting the d-pawn and the c1-square.

Putting all this data into considerations, is there a move that Black can unleash to send White's defence into disarray? The question right away leads Black's attention to focus on the d- and e-pawns, which are the weakest points in White's formation. The motif of removing the defender delivers decisive play as demonstrated by Black's next move. Even an elite grandmaster rated at 2609 falls victim to the alert exploitation of combined weaknesses and proper use of a tactical motif:

39...♗xd4!

(see following diagram)

40 ♕xd4

40 ♗xd4 loses to 40...♕c1+ 41 ♔a2 ♖c2+.

40...♕c2+ 0-1

White resigns.

Notice how the poor coordination between the knight and rook combined with the weak central pawns became White's undoing.

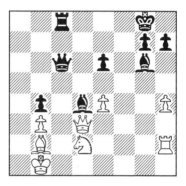

Game 20
V.Ivanchuk-T.Radjabov
Wijk aan Zee 2009
King's Indian Defence

1 d4 ♘f6 2 c4 g6 3 ♘c3 ♗g7 4 e4 d6 5 ♗e2 0-0 6 ♘f3 e5 7 0-0 ♘c6 8 d5 ♘e7 9 b4 ♘e8 10 a4 f5 11 a5 ♘f6 12 ♗g5 ♘h5 13 exf5 gxf5 14 ♕d2 ♘f6 15 c5 ♗d7 16 b5 ♗e8 17 c6 b6 18 ♘h4 ♗f7 19 ♗d3 ♗g6 20 f3 ♕e8 21 ♔h1 ♔h8 22 ♗c2 ♕f7 23 g4 ♘fg8 24 ♖a4 ♖ae8 25 axb6 axb6 26 ♖a7 ♖c8 27 ♘xg6+ ♕xg6 28 ♖g1 ♕f7 29 ♖g3 e4 30 ♘e2 ♘f6 31 ♘f4 exf3 32 gxf5 ♘fxd5 33 ♖xf3 ♘xf4 34 ♕xf4 ♗f6 35 ♗b3 ♕h5 36 ♗xf6+ ♖xf6 37 ♗e6

The bishop threatens to capture the rook on c8. An indirect threat is to munch the c7-pawn after the black rook moves away to a safer square.

37...♖cf8

If you were playing White, what would you do after Black's last move? Does Black have a threat? Doing a proper reconnaissance of the position would yield an even more serious threat which White could not afford to ignore.

Black must have expected White to play something like 38 ♗d7. White failed to do a simple reconnaissance of the resulting position and simply carried out his threat against the pawn operating on the basis of old data. I am sure Black could not believe his eyes when he saw White's unexpected move:

38 ♖xc7??

Black, for sure, still a little discomfited by White's generosity, accepted the unexpected booty next move. Now we see that even super-grandmasters can make this kind of mistake once in a while. Black's previous move not only nullified White's threat of winning the c7-pawn, but it also carried an even bigger threat of winning White's bishop.

38...♖xe6

This captures the bishop and protects the knight. Meanwhile, the pawn cannot recapture on e6 because it is pinned to his queen. In the game, White felt obliged to take the rook and gave up his queen, but resigned three moves later:

39 fxe6 ♖xf4 40 ♖xf4 ♕d5+ 41 ♔g1 ♕g5+ 0-1

The question regarding the viability of the system lingers even in my own mind, since evidence is severely lacking. It is accepted wisdom that only data sets in the form of expected outcomes can verify the correctness of any process. Truly convinced of its efficacy, I proceeded to map out plans for collecting the desired proof. In order to subject my system to its most severe tests and to preclude outlier results I thought it was best that I become the controlled subject and marshal its unveiling in the hostile world of norm events where I would be the lowest-rated player among the company of titled players seeking norms for even higher titles.

The remaining chapters of the book will tell you the rest of the story.

Chapter Three

New England Masters, August 2008

In August 2008, I bravely or rather foolishly entered the New England Masters in Pawtucket, Rhode Island. The field consisted of 44 players (including 4 GMS, 8 IMs, 11 FMs and 1 WFM) representing 12 federations. My singular purpose of playing in this event was to secure evidence in the form of data points for my blunder-proof system and to confirm the hypothesis that one can improve in chess at any age as long as he is armed with the right resources, empowered with effortful study, inspired with the right attitude, and enabled with the right thinking process.

My excitement reached its zenith when after five rounds I had scored 3 points: two wins and two draws against titled players. My rating performance after five rounds was 2373. I survived two full days of play without a loss. In the critical round six, I was paired up against IM Sarkar who already had one GM norm and had narrowly missed one more. Despite my loss to him I was still at even score and my rating performance remained high at 2322. I just needed to play three more games against FIDE-rated combatants averaging 2300 and score 1½ for an initial rating high enough to earn the FIDE Master title. How improbable would that be? For sure, it would be viewed either as a fluke or a breakthrough. At the very least, it would challenge the prevailing notion that adult players hardly improve in chess. A number of players intoned that I would definitely get a high rating and possibly even a FIDE Master title in this tournament if I could maintain my performance for a couple more rounds. The comments were made with hints of puzzled wonderment over my unrated status. My good fortunes bothered rather than helped me in the last four rounds.

Because of my score I kept getting paired up, this time against IM Hungaski who had a rating of 2407. This uneven matchup indicated how the titled players were faring in the field and how well I was doing. When the October 2008 FIDE list was published, I received an initial international rating of 2199.

My opponent in the first round was a young Canadian FIDE Master, who already had one IM norm and had just came off fresh from beating the former US Champion, GM Alexander Shabalov. In October 2009 at the 80th FIDE Congress in Greece, my opponent was awarded the IM title.

Game 21
A.Hortillosa-R.Panjwani
Pawtucket 2008
English Opening

1 c4 b6 2 ♘c3 c5 3 ♘f3 ♗b7 4 e4 e6 5 d4 cxd4 6 ♘xd4 a6 7 ♗e2

A very flexible set-up is 7 ♕e2 d6 8 g3 ♘f6 9 ♗g2, and this has been played in numerous games.

7...♕c7

Black can also play 7...d6 8 0-0 ♘f6 9 f3 ♘bd7 10 ♗e3 ♗e7.

8 a3 ♘f6

Here I diverged from theory (9 f3) not by choice but because of deficient knowledge of theory.

9 ♕c2 ♗e7 10 ♗e3 d6 11 0-0 ♘bd7 12 f4

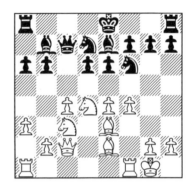

During the game I thought this move was too aggressive but it's true to my style. I love taking space if given the opportunity. IM Ginsburg, who was my coach at this time, confirmed in a short phone conversation later that evening that the move has merit and in fact he's played it himself. I wish we had had time to look at the Hedgehog before the event because it would have given me enough guideposts to find my way around without falling into a bad position.

12...0-0 13 ♖ac1

It is always a good idea when there are no other pressing matters needing attention on the board to shadow the queen with a rook. But continuing on with the idea of attacking Black directly, g2-g4 keeps the initiative. Believe it or not, if Black is allowed time to do it, the seemingly weakening ...h5 is one of the many active ideas he can pursue in this position. In fact, we briefly analyzed it during the postmortem. IM Ginsburg provided good coverage of the ideas behind the move

13...♖ac8 14 b4 ♕b8 15 ♕b1 ♕a8

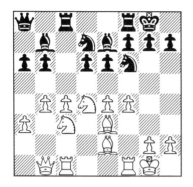

The engines judge the position to be equal. Note Black's set-up in case you want to play along the same path against 1 c4. The transfer of the queen to a8 is a standard manoeuvre. This became possible only because I did not continue actively with g2-g4 and g4-g5. A better version of my set-up would have been to post the queen on d3 to shore up the defence of c4 while keeping the queen along the b1-h7 diagonal. I was still hoping to commence an assault against the Black king. The other merit of ♕d3 is the natural access the queen gets to the third rank.

16 ♗d3

This move cedes control of the g4-square to Black, which he immediately took and induced disharmony on my pieces. However, I was left with very little choice as I had to defend the e4-pawn somehow.

16...♘g4 17 ♗d2

An active-looking defence in 17 ♖f3 looks playable but I rejected it because at the minimum White gets into a bit of a mess as he is forced to give up his dark-squared bishop for the black knight. Everywhere in this book I emphasize the importance of nullifying or falsifying your own move before making it on the board as another effective way of limiting blunders. Questions to ask yourself might be: What can he do to refute my move? Or what is wrong with this move?

17...b5

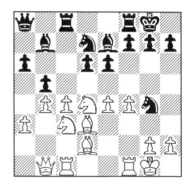

18 ♘c2??

This move forfeits any advantage I had. It might be difficult to believe but I was in serious time trouble here. The decision to play 18 ♘c2 was based on what I thought I had seen earlier. One of the lines I had examined and judged to be harmful for me was a check with ...♕a7 followed by...♘f2+ winning the exchange. When in time trouble, we tend to make our moves in a reflexive manner, which are based not on concrete variations but stored information. Since the text move loses a pawn without compensation, White should have entered the complications arising after 18 cxb5.

18...bxc4

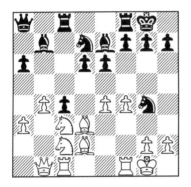

It went downhill from here on. I lost on time before I could make my 33rd move, but the game was already beyond saving anyway. My young opponent after the game kindly told me to avoid spending too much time trying to find the best moves because with this time control second-rate moves are sometimes good enough. I took note and heeded his wise advice in the later rounds.

The rest of the game went as follows:

19 ♗e2 ♘gf6 20 ♗f3 ♘xe4 21 ♘xe4 ♗xe4 22 ♗c3 ♗f6 23 ♕b2 ♗xc3 24 ♕xc3 ♘f6 25 ♖ce1 ♕a7+ 26 ♔h1 ♗d3 27 ♖g1 ♗xc2 28 ♕xc2 d5 29 f5 exf5 30 ♕xf5 ♖fd8 31 g4 d4 32 g5 ♘e8 0-1

After this first-round loss, I began to wonder about my decision to test my wares with the big boys. That evening when I went over the game I noted that the error on move 18 was not caused by a system failure. The error was

mostly due to my misapplication of the system at critical points of the game. You see I am also a consumer of my own chess thinking process. The more I apply it the better I play. With my unwavering confidence in the system undisturbed, I resolved to be more diligent in my reliance to its soundness in the next rounds.

Game 22
L.Belliard-A.Hortillosa
Pawtucket 2008
Nimzo-Indian Defence

1 d4 ♘f6 2 c4 e6 3 ♘c3 ♗b4 4 ♕c2 ♘c6

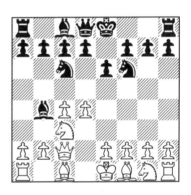

This was the first time I employed the Zurich Variation against 4 ♕c2 in a tournament game. Before the tournament, I ordered IM Vigorito's excellent book *Challenging the Nimzo Indian* hoping to get much needed theoretical foundation on this particular line. But the book arrived literally only days before the tournament so I never got a chance to really delve into it. Although I am familiar with the general plans for Black, my theoretical knowledge of the main lines before this game was next to nothing. I admit it was a reckless tournament strategy and foolhardy too.

The first time I saw the line played was in one of GM Perelshteyn's games. I liked the middlegame plans arising out of the line so I made it into my main defence against White's solid ♕c2 set-up.

5 ♘f3 0-0

Another good option for Black is to delay castling and play 5...d6 retaining some flexibility.

6 a3 ♗xc3+ 7 ♕xc3 d6 8 ♗g5 ♕e7

A tempting continuation is to harass the bishop with 8...h6 9 ♗h4 g5 10 ♗g3 ♘e4 11 ♕c2 f5 12 e3 ♕f6 when Black has gained space on the kingside and is ahead in development. In contrast, White has yet to complete his development.

9 e3 e5 10 d5 ♘b8 11 ♗e2 ♘bd7 12 0-0 a5

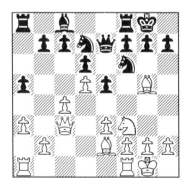

If Black wishes to plant a knight on

c5, one way of ensuring that it will not get dislodged from the nice outpost by a pawn is to play ...a5. If White prepares b2-b4 with a2-a3, then Black should play ...a5-a4 and capture en passant when White plays b2-b4. In this case the pawn on a3 would become weak, Black would get a half-open a-file and White's lever c4-c5 would be harder to engineer. The usual method of combating Black's idea is for White to play b2-b3 before playing a2-a3. The idea is to reply with b3-b4 when Black plays ...a5-a4. Remember this motif because you will see it in other set-ups. One such set-up is seen when Black plays on the dark squares against the Maroczy Bind.

13 ♘d2 ♖e8

I played 13...♖e8 with the idea of answering 14 ♘e4?? with 14...♘xe4. If the bishop takes the queen on e7, I can answer with ...♘xc3 and Black wins a piece. With the rook no longer on f8, the bishop has nothing to capture and must retreat. If White takes the knight on c3, Black wins the bishop on e7.

14 ♕c2 h6

I should first take care of the queenside by playing 14...a4 while I have the chance before embarking on a kingside expansion. The knight on d7 must be redeployed to a better post to give the light-squared bishop some scope and a quick entrance into the game as necessary.

15 ♗h4 g5

Once again, Black should first secure a knight outpost on c5 with 15...a4 before escalating any aggression on the kingside while there is opportunity. After 16 ♔h1, chances are even.

16 ♗g3 e4

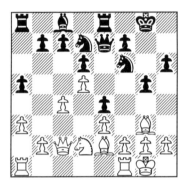

I had been considering ...a5-a4 on the previous two moves but when the opportunity to play ...e5-e4 arose, I took it before White could play e3-e4 himself. While ...a5-a4 secures a knight outpost on c5, advancing the pawn to e4 gives me a better outpost on e5.

17 b4 b6

In my other games with the Nimzo-Indian, I have shown a strong preference for slowing down White's c4-c5 advance on the queenside. It is not necessary to do so here, but old biases are hard to resist. Besides, I had correctly thought that White had nothing immediate that would translate to wresting the initiative.

18 ♘b3

I could have prevented this move with 17...a4, but I wasn't afraid of the knight reaching d4.

18...♘e5 19 ♕c3

My chess engines like 19 bxa5 bxa5 20 ♘d4 bestowing some edge to White.

19...a4 20 ♘d4

The problem with the e-pawn advance is losing control of d4, which White can use as entry point into Black's camp. But since f5 is protected, the square is littered with mines waiting for intruders with bad intentions.

20...♗d7

When making this move, I recalled GM Aagaard's sage advice in his *Attacking Manual* to always include under-worked pieces in the attack whenever possible.

21 ♖fd1

I am not sure if the rook should leave the f-file. White should instead consider 21 ♖ac1.

21...h5

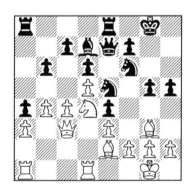

I already started feeling optimistic about my position. During the game I thought I had seized the initiative here with this pawn advance, but chess engines could only confirm equality and nothing more.

22 h4

Very committal.

22...♞fg4

I was not sure if my opponent expected this move, but he gave enough clues that he didn't judging by his demeanour and his use of time over his next moves.

23 hxg5 ♕xg5 24 c5

White is forced to initiate active operations on this side of the board. He cannot just wait for Black's attack on the kingside to develop. If White plays, 24 ♗f4 the obvious 24...♕g6 equalizes.

24...♚h7

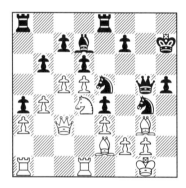

I felt I should directly attack the king before White could consolidate so I vacated the g-file providing access for the rooks. Another solid option is the expansion in the kingside with 24...h4 25 ♗f4 ♕g6 26 cxd6 cxd6 27 ♕c7 when both sides should be happy in reaching a lively position with equal chances to play for a win.

25 cxd6

White took over 15 minutes to decide on this move. I could tell he was unhappy with his position. Observing your opponent's face for tells has some benefits. If you see obvious discomfort, cheer up and search for what is bothering your opponent. Just be careful because some are just bad actors.

25...cxd6 26 ♞c6?

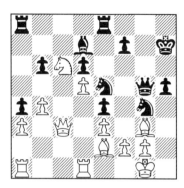

I was happy to see this move. Not all outposts are good. The new squares influenced by the knight on c6 are no more critical than those it touched while perched on d4. I guess 26 ♞c6 was more of an anticipatory move aimed at defusing the rook's pressure along the c-file. It's also possible that White simply wanted to exchange twice on e5 for the purpose of removing threatening attackers in the vicinity of his king.

A much better choice is 26 ♕c2 ♕g6 27 ♗h4, which keeps the balance.

26...♖g8

After this move, the engines are heavily favouring Black.

27 ♗f4?

This move does not do much for White except make the king more insecure. Now the only cover standing between the queen and rook battery and White's king is the knight on g4.

Worth considering is 27 ♘xe5!? but after 27...dxe5 28 ♗f1 Black still retains some advantage and the initiative.

27...♕g7

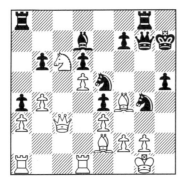

Played instantly. The most obvious threat is against the undefended queen on c3.

28 ♔f1?

The king shuffle to f1 removes the present danger to the queen from the discovered attack ...♘f3+. I could tell that my opponent was deeply worried by that threat more than any danger resulting from the ...♘xf2 invasion.

Against 28 ♕e1 Black has the clearing manoeuvre 28...♘xe3! winning a pawn and the exchange after 29 g3 ♘xd1.

28...♖ac8?

The question mark is for unreasonable hesitation. I spent over 30 minutes deciding which way to continue but settled on this pragmatic choice based on the following deliberations. I wanted to be sure of victory so I

thought the text move was necessary to seal off the white king's escape route via the c-file. Psychology was at play here.

The immediate and decisive 28...♘xf2 wins on the spot. White has two moves but both are losing:

a) 29 ♘xe5 ♖ac8 30 ♕d4 ♕xg2+ 31 ♔e1 ♖c2 32 ♖d2 ♕g1+ 33 ♗f1 dxe5 34 ♕xb6 ♘d3+ 35 ♖xd3 ♕f2+ 36 ♔d1 ♗g4+ with mate to follow.

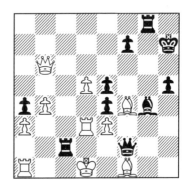

b) 29 ♗xe5 ♕xg2+ 30 ♔e1 ♘xd1 31 ♖xd1 dxe5 32 ♕xe5 with Black winning the exchange and a pawn.

29 ♕d4??

The double question mark is for underestimating Black's possibilities. I was relieved to see this move appear on the board. I was right to guess that the knight sacrifice on f2 never showed up on White's radar.

A better try is 29 g3 ♘xf2 30 ♔xf2 ♘g4+ 31 ♔xg4 ♕xc3 32 ♗xd7 ♕b2+ 33 ♔f1 when although Black has the advantage, all routes to the white king are still securely protected.

29...♘xf2!

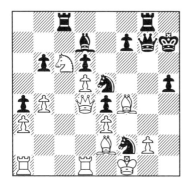

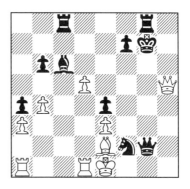

Played forcefully and with a lot of confidence. I was certain I was already winning here.

30 ♗xe5

This move only worsens the situation. A sturdier defensive try is 30 g3 ♘xd1 31 ♖xd1 ♘xc6 32 ♕xe4+ ♕g6 33 ♕xg6+ fxg6 34 dxc6 ♖xc6 35 ♗f3, but Black remains on top.

30...♕xg2+ 31 ♔e1 dxe5 32 ♕xe5 ♗xc6?!

A much safer continuation which doesn't allow any counterplay is 32...♖g5 when play might continue as in 33 ♕e7 ♕g1+ 34 ♔d2 ♖xd5+ 35 ♘d4 ♕g7 36 ♖g1 ♖xd4+ 37 exd4 ♕xd4+ 38 ♔e1 ♕xa1+ 39 ♔xf2 ♕d4+, with Black winning.

White was getting low on time so he saved some precious seconds with a check. I was so upset with myself for allowing this capture and check.

33 ♕xh5+

33 ♕f5+ ♖g6 34 ♕xf7+ ♔h6 35 ♕xf2 ♕xf2+ 36 ♔xf2 ♖f8+ is also hopeless for White.

33...♔g7 0-1

White lost on time anyway, but Black is still clearly winning. Not a bad try for my first outing with 4...♘c6. This win was liberating because the pressure was lifted off my shoulders. The fear of scoring a perfect zero left without saying goodbye. I could hardly contain my excitement over the possibilities. Chris Bird, the ever genial British expat who served as arbiter and organizer of the tournament, was happy for me too. I felt invigorated for the next round of the day, against a player who had already achieved two international master norms.

> ### Game 23
> ### A.Hortillosa-N.Castaneda
> ### Pawtucket 2008
> ### *King's Indian Defence*

IM Ginsburg and I had one good session on the Classical Variation against the King's Indian Defence. Most of my openings for this tournament were new to my repertoire. I hired IM

Ginsburg to specifically retool my tattered opening repertoire. I realized that playing the main lines of major openings is the only way to go if someone like me hopes to ever get to fight on a slightly more even field against stronger players. My preparation for the popular KID is the line you are about to see.

By the way, it is worth mentioning that I virtually always play the Torre Attack against the Grünfeld and King's Indian set-ups. In fact, I pretty much rely on the Torre Attack against most Black set-ups, especially when Black's first move is 1...♘f6.

1 c4

I wanted to play against the King's Indian but wished to avoid most of Black's other defences such as the Grünfeld, Benko and the Benoni, so I opened the game as such. The only problem with this move order is the possibility for Black to decline the offer of entering the King's Indian and play instead any of the following: 1...c5, 1...e5 or 1...f5.

1...♘f6

Good. I was happy that my opponent was cooperating. You see, I was anxious to try out my preparation against the King's Indian.

2 ♘c3 g6 3 e4 d6 4 d4 ♗g7 5 ♘f3

This is book, but strong grandmasters would sometimes prefer 5 ♗e2. The moves ♗e2 and ♘f3 can be interchanged, but developing the bishop before the knight removes one playable

option for Black in ...♗g4. More than the majority of King's Indian players prefer keeping the light-squared bishop because in most lines this bishop provides essential support to the kingside pawn advance and it projects influential control on the critical h3- and g4-squares in White's camp from a distance. You could say this piece is already developed on its original square. You will seldom find experienced King's Indian practitioners moving this piece to another square. Indeed, set-ups where the parting of this bishop is beneficial to Black are rare, and one of these is seen in this game.

5...0-0 6 ♗e2 e5

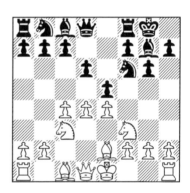

Doesn't this move lose a pawn for Black? Elsewhere in this book I emphasize more than once the need to figure out why strong players play certain moves. Most improvers especially those new to the King's Indian would think that Black has just blundered a pawn. Before we establish whether he indeed did or did not, let's embark on a worthy digression.

Now let's assume you are unfamiliar with theory, how would you continue as White? One side benefit of my system is its inherent ability to guide you through the maze of complications probably unscathed from lurking traps in the opening. Or, as in this instance, simply help you dismiss a continuation on the grounds that better opportunities lay just ahead.

Let's explore this some more by doing the now familiar exercise. First, let's do a general reconnaissance of the position after Black's last move. The first thing to notice is the hostile contact between the e5-pawn and the d4-pawn. Second, White has the option of taking on e5 twice and the extra option of exchanging queens in between captures. Mind you, the line starting with 7 dxe5 is playable, but is that what you want as White? If White believes he is winning a pawn, he may indeed continue with the line which begins with 7 dxe5.

So let's see if the system will enable the White player, who does not know theory specific to the position, ascertain the worthiness of the capture on e5.

If White castles with 7 0-0 as in the game, Black has the threat of capturing on d4 with 7...exd4. A standard system inquiry to consider is whether White can simply ignore the threat. The answer, of course, is yes because White can advantageously recapture on d4 with 8 ♘xd4. It centralizes the knight

and castling before the recapture has positively placed him ahead in development. Seeing no serious black threats, White in a systematic fashion checks (left to right) the battle terrain if he has a threat he can execute leading to a material advantage. Seeing that the e5-pawn is defended only once by the d6-pawn but is attacked twice by the d4-pawn and knight on f3, White might conclude that he can win a pawn starting with the sequence 7 dxe5, the move under consideration.

Following through with the system we can establish 7 dxe5 as a plausible candidate. After the capture on e5, it is easy to see that Black is forced to respond with 7...dxe5 to establish material parity. From here the game likely may continue with 8 ♕xd8 ♖xd8 9 ♘xe5 temporarily winning a pawn. I say temporarily because Black has 9...♘xe4 regaining the pawn. Notice the changes in the battle terrain.

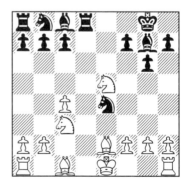

The white knight on e5 is attacked by the bishop on g7. If White continues with 10 ♘xe4, Black responds with

10...♗xe5 leading to equality. Upon arriving at the above diagram in his calculation, White may also get tempted by the desperado 10 ♘xf7 thinking it will force Black to capture the knight with his king because on f7 it threatens to capture the vulnerable rook on d8. He reasons this will buy him time to capture the proffered knight on e4 netting him a pawn in the process.

But yet again the standard system inquiry asking if Black can ignore White's threat with his own threat would yield the forcing 10...♗xc3+, which effectively falsifies White's threat against the rook on d8. After the forced 11 bxc3, it is Black who will emerge with material gain after 11...♔xf7 winning the knight for a pawn. If White is judicious in his application of the system, he succeeds in preventing a blunder and discovers that the most he can get from the candidate 7 dxe5 is equality. Knowing better, White may then wisely decide to search for an advantage elsewhere.

Some specific opening knowledge like the one above is indispensable as it saves precious time and energy. Experienced players on the White side of the King's Indian are well acquainted with this kind of error. But in the absence of this knowledge, a formalized chess thinking process is your next best substitute.

7 0-0

The text is the universal choice of strong players. Not only that it tucks the king away into safety, it also makes the threat of winning a pawn real because now the ensuing capture on c3 no longer comes with check. Does White have to be concerned about 7...exd4? No. True King's Indian players do not capture on d4 because that would change the pawn structure into something atypical of the desired King's Indian pawn formation in the centre.

7...♘c6 8 d5

White waits until Black adds pressure on d4 with ...♘c6 before playing the text move. It "tempos" the knight and forces it to move away from the centre. Black is happy to oblige because he wants the knight to get to e7 anyway to help support the ...f5 advance later. The knight can get closer to White's king via e7 to g6.

8 d5 ♘e7 9 b4

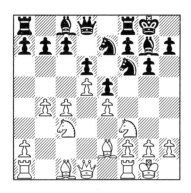

When you add a new opening to your repertoire, pick one or two main lines and limit your acquisition of theoretical knowledge to these lines. *As a*

practical matter, players like us are best served by going deeper not wider in our repertoire build-up.

One effective way of really learning and understanding an opening line is to collect games using the filter function in ChessBase of strong players known for their regular employment of the chosen line. There are hundreds of players who have successfully learned their openings by playing over games of masters and not from an opening monograph. Limit your search to games of players with Elo rating no lower than 2350. You can further limit your collection to games played in the last 20 years. If you are willing to pay for it, you can subscribe to services like that of *ChessPublishing.com* where you can subscribe to one of the twelve opening subscripting services. The grandmaster or international master who is responsible for writing the monthly updates normally uses the most current games to showcase the most current fashion. You can also grow and update the database with newer games from other sources like *The Week in Chess* for free. Try to add your own notes or comments you read from books directly into the games. Once you have the games, simply re-play them over at normal speed to get a general feel of how the games progress. This gives you a comprehensive idea of how strong players continue from the initial set-up.

9...♘h5

Black wants to play ...f7-f5 but the knight on f6 hinders the advance, thus the rationale behind the knight hop to h5.

10 c5

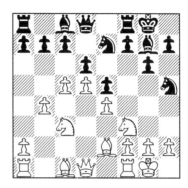

This is officially the start of the line I had prepared for. I could tell that my opponent was not expecting it. It took him almost 15 minutes to decide on his response.

My move is not new, just old. Castaneda was only making sure he was not getting into unfamiliar territory. My choice is hardly played these days because of the preference for Kramnik's 10 ♖e1. Another older alternative to the now standard 10 ♖e1 is 10 g3, making f4 inhabitable for the knight. That too has fallen into ill-repute because the pawn advance to g3 comes at a steep price in exchange for the gain it buys. For one, it weakens the light squares in front of the king. But a more serious drawback is the faster contact the advance facilitates with Black's f- or h-pawn. With the pawn now on g3, it will take two moves instead of three for the f-pawn to effect a file-opening exchange advantageous to Black's agenda.

The main idea of 10 ♖e1 is to make room for the bishop after ...♘f4. White allows the landing on f4 arguing that the knight only impedes Black's standard pawn avalanche. Since it cannot capture on e2 with check after the bishop retreats to f1, Black will be forced to waste a crucial tempo in moving the knight to open the way for the marauding pawns.

10...♘f4 11 ♗xf4

The tempo-gaining move is key to White's plan. White wants to move the bishop off c1 with tempo and Black has provided the opportunity since a recapture is mandatory.

11...exf4 12 ♖c1

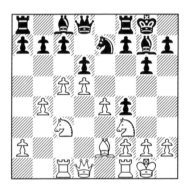

Now White's rook is watchfully influencing the c-file, ready to dominate once it gets opened. White is faster on the queenside than Black is on the kingside as many master games have shown. The plan is clear and easy to carry out.

12...a5

It is my turn to get surprised as I was not expecting this at all, though I have seen it played in a couple of high-profile games. Black normally continues with 12...h6 followed by ...g6-g5.

13 cxd6

I later asked IM Ginsburg what to do here over the phone, anticipating seeing it again in the same tournament. He said White should maintain the chain with 13 a3, but I am not sure if White should help Black develop his rook on a8 if he answers with ...axb4. I have to defer to him because he knows this line very well.

13...cxd6 14 ♘b5

This will tie up the queen to the defence of d6. With 14 ♘b5 White exploits the absence of a pawn on both adjacent files able to drive the knight away. My game almost plays itself whereas Black is struggling to come up with a decent plan. The speed of my invasion on the queenside will keep Black busy there and he will never get a chance to get his own attack on the kingside going. But there is one last thing he can do to improve his chances and he was apt for it.

14...♗g4!

This is how Kasparov continued in his game against Kamsky. It is somewhat surprising that my chess engines adjudged the position to be equal. Is this an example of a positional advantage that computers cannot evaluate correctly?

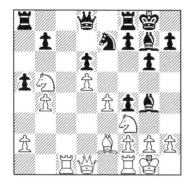

With 14...♗g4, Black is signalling that he no longer aspires to pushing his kingside pawns. It should have given me pause and I should have taken the time to figure out Black's intentions. What does he want? I didn't know because I didn't ask. *If you do not ask, you will never look. And if you do not look, you will not find as well.*

15 bxa5

Much better is 15 ♘d2. Black should never be allowed to exchange his bishop for the knight, as the knights are important for the attack on the queenside.

Kamsky opted for 15 ♖c7 in G.Kamsky-G.Kasparov, New York (rapid) 1996. Let's see the rest of the game: 15...axb4 16 ♕d2 ♗xf3 17 ♗xf3 ♗e5 18 ♖xb7 ♕a5 19 ♘d4 ♕xa2 20 ♕xa2 ♖xa2 21 ♖xb4 ♖fa8 22 ♗g4 ♗xd4 23 ♖xd4 g5 24 h4 gxh4 25 ♔h2 ♘g6 26 ♔h3 ♖b2 27 ♗f5 ♘e5 28 ♔xh4 h6 29 ♗h3 ♔g7 (Kasparov's pieces are more active than Kamsky's, and a mating net is also forming around White's king) 30 ♖dd1 ♖aa2 31 f3 ♘g6+ 32 ♔g4 ♔f6 33 ♖b1

h5+ 34 ♔xh5 ♖a8 35 ♔g4 ♖h8 36 g3 ♖h2 37 ♖h1 ♖8xh3 38 ♖xh2 ♖xh2 39 gxf4 ♖g2+ 40 ♔h3 ♘xf4+ 41 ♔h4 ♔e5 42 ♖b7 ♔d4 43 ♖xf7 ♔e3 0-1.

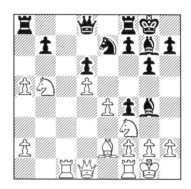

15...♗xf3

Black answered my equivocation immediately. The knight would control more squares on the queenside than the bishop. Black was quick to recognize this. The trade rendered my bishop even less effective than before. It was just now that I understood the point of Black's ...♗g4 move. Even after my knight's demise, I thought of its commanding presence on d4. If the exchange was to be allowed, it should have been for Black's dark-squared bishop.

Silman's thoughts on imbalances really sound loud on positions like this one. Had I taken the time to recon the landscape, I would have seen which imbalance to rid of fast in exchange for a better one. The benefit of annotating your games is first knowing, then reinforcing and finally storing such chess knowledge for future use. The benefit of playing over model master games like the Kamsky-Kasparov encounter is seeing to the point of acquiring familiarity with similar motifs.

16 ♗xf3 ♖xa5 17 a4

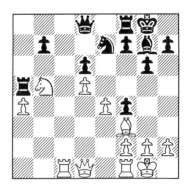

When I took on a5 I was on my own. Over the board I saw the possibility of organizing a set-up with ♕b3, ♖c7, ♖fc1 and ♗d1 as a winning battle formation for White.

17...♕b6?!

Black's queen has no future on b6. It will only get harassed by White's rooks. The possibility of the queen getting trapped will gain White some tempi as Black expends time extricating it to safety. The queen sortie on b6 does not come without its own nasty trap, which to my credit I saw right away.

A better option for Black is 17...♘c8 18 ♕b3 and the game stands equal.

18 ♖c4

Anticipating Black's next move. Black's plan is wrong-headed as the concentration of his pieces in the corner would only create a logjam.

18 ♖c7 is bad because of 18...♖xb5

19 ♖xe7 ♖b2 when my rook on e7 is stranded helpless on the seventh rank whereas Black's is active. Just like that and Black has seized the advantage. This was the position Black was hoping for with his 17th move.

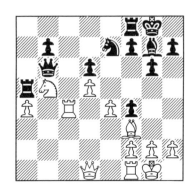

18...♖fa8

18...♖c8 is a faster route to equality. The text gives White a slight advantage after taking control of the open c-file.

19 ♕c2 ♗f6

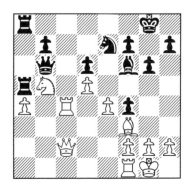

Black is running out of constructive moves. The knight has no square and will require defence when the white rook penetrates on the seventh rank. My coach tells me to always labour to understand your opponent's plans. So here I wondered what Black was up to besides simply defending the knight. I could play the rook to b1 or c1 immediately but after seeing that Black was planning to bring his king to g7, I thought of how I could take advantage of the king's position on that square. I gave Black a free move with 20 h3. This just shows that White has the edge because he can afford to make moves like h2-h3, though one can also forward a valid argument that it gives luft to his king just in case.

20 h3 ♔g7

This was Black's last chance to extricate the queen with 20...♕d8!?.

21 ♘c7

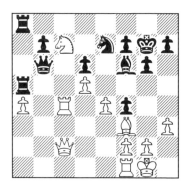

Securing the advantage for White. Because the king is now on g7, Black cannot reroute the rook to c8 as it would surrender its dear life to a discovered check with ♘e6+. Now I have a simple winning plan involving lining up my rooks and queen against the b7-pawn, protecting the a-pawn with ♗d1 and capturing Black's b-pawn.

21...♖d8 22 ♖b1 ♕a7 23 ♖cb4?

One careless move and Black escapes prison and gains some activity.

A more decisive move and almost winning is 23 ♘b5!. Now that the queen is driven into the corner and the rook is bearing down on the b-file, the knight should return to again imprison the rook. This retreating move is hard to see, and training one's positional eyes to spot these manoeuvre types will bring net dividends to one's playing ability. Play might continue as in 23...♕a8 24 ♗d1 ♗e5 25 ♖c7 ♔f8 26 ♕d2 b6 27 ♖bc1 ♖c8 28 ♕c2 ♖b8 with White retaining a big advantage.

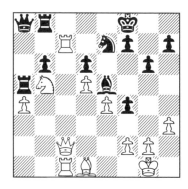

White should be winning here because the d-pawn will get surrounded and will eventually fall. Meanwhile, the rook on a5 and the black queen have very little scope.

23...♖c5

Black was quick to take advantage of White's lapse and is now poised to strike back and reactivate the queen. White's advantage has disappeared after one careless move.

24 ♘b5

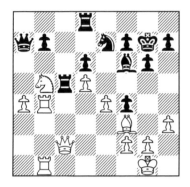

24...♕a5

24...♖xc2 simplifies Black's drawing task but he rejected it most likely due to a fear of losing his b-pawn. After 25 ♘xa7 ♘c8 26 ♘b5, the balance is again restored.

25 ♕e2

Much better is 25 ♕d1 keeping contact with the a-pawn while controlling the c1-square.

25...♗e5 26 ♘a3 ♖c1+

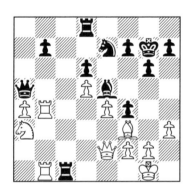

27 ♔h2

Good thing I took the time for a luft. When is a good time to make a luft? The best time to make a luft is before you need it! Kidding aside, you know it is the best time when making it does not allow your opponent to steal the initiative from you and when there is some quiet on the board.

I considered 27 ♖xc1 but I evaluated the position incorrectly. It turned out I was really afraid of nothing. I saw Black continuing with 27...♕xb4 28 ♘c4 ♖c8 and it was Black's last move I was afraid of during my over-the-board thinking. I overlooked the possibility of 29 ♕f1 maintaining contact with the rook on c1.

27...♖xb1 28 ♖xb1 ♕xa4 29 ♘c4

The pawn on b7 is going nowhere. Black gains the advantage after the inferior 29 ♖xb7 ♕xa3 30 ♖xe7 ♕c1.

29...♖b8 30 ♘xe5 dxe5

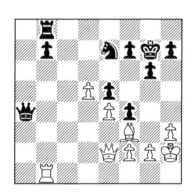

Now White has his own passed pawn. The ending, if it gets there, will be good for White.

31 ♕b2 f6

Black can easily hold the draw, but I was not sure if my opponent was playing for a win because he had declined one draw offer earlier. Black could also try 31...♕d4 32 ♕c2 ♖c8 33 ♕a2 and the game is equal.

32 ♕b6

If 32 ♕c3, then 32...♕d7 maintains the balance.

32...♕d7 33 ♕a7 ♕c7 34 ♖b6 ♘c8

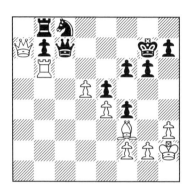

In our post-mortem analysis, Black said he thought he was winning here and that I had blundered the rook.

35 ♖c6

The only move and this forces a draw.

35...♕xc6 36 ♕xb8 ♕c5 37 ♕xb7+ ♔h6

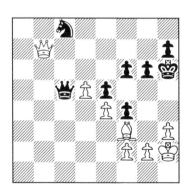

38 ♕c6

White could try 38 ♕b2 but still reeling from a letdown on move 23,

which allowed Black back into the game, I was not emotionally ready to keep on playing. The upside is I scored 1½ points in one day.

38...♕xf2 ½-½

Draw agreed.

Game 24
C.Galofre-A.Hortillosa
Pawtucket 2008
Réti Opening

Before this encounter, I searched my database wanting to know my opponent's preferred opening as White. Let's just say I did some pretty good pre-game reconnaissance of the future battlefield.

1 ♘f3

I noticed my young opponent's propensity towards this ultra-flexible move. Amateurs like us have really not considered transpositions and move-order tricks as a necessary fixture in our limited arsenal. We tend to think that transpositions are the sole province of titled players and professionals. My research elicited some measure of confidence never before seen in my tournament experience. You see, like you I decide on my opening set-up based on what I see on the board and not before. Preferably, opening formations must be decided prior to the game because the habit of doing so dictates some formality on your game preparation. It saves time as well, which is better spent during the critical junctures of the game rather than while the terrain of the battlefield is yet to be established.

1...♘f6

Black has a rich choice of responses but this move is equally flexible as White's. Neither side is willing this early to reveal his preferred formation.

2 c4

Most amateurs do not understand or care to understand the point of White's move order. If you invest study time on this, your opening choices will suddenly make sense. At the very least, you will experience some clarity on why you open your game this way or that way.

2...e6 3 g3

White can no longer hide his intended set-up. Any other move will lead to something not necessarily markedly different, but different nevertheless to a specific set-up my opponent revels in playing. Some players only like to play a certain way in their favourite backyard because terrain familiarity brings safety and comfort.

3...a6

I got this idea from IM Palliser's book, *Beating Unusual Chess Openings*. Black delays kingside development in exchange for the initiative and queenside development.

4 ♗g2 b5

Anytime contact between chessmen occurs, the player on the move has the onus to either ignore or react. I like

Black's idea here because as early as move three he is imposing his will on the White player, which in itself precipitates a mental burden forcing White to spend energy and time resources. 3...a6 and 4...b5 disrupts the usual flow in White's development. Very early, he is forced to respond to something other than what he is accustomed to. This can be disconcerting to some players who are used to only playing to their own tunes. I get about the same feeling when someone plays ...c5 on the first move against 1 d4. I usually feel that Black is unwilling to cooperate into playing something familiar. It used to annoy me until I came up with something designed to annoy back.

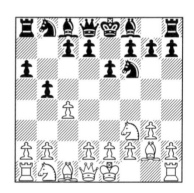

5 b3

White correctly avoids the exchange of his c-pawn for the less valuable b-pawn by protecting it. The move also readies the development of the bishop to b2 eyeing a critical diagonal.

5...c5

This move is a critical follow-up to

Black's opening sequence. The problem with ...b5 is that it necessitates ...c5 so as to provide access to b6 for the queen in case White attacks b5 with ♘c3, as played in the game. I believe this is the most important point for Black to remember in this set-up. The rest of the moves should come in a more incidental way if you wish to describe it. In a sense, that is the extent of your opening preparation: very efficient and also economical.

6 ♘c3 ♛b6 7 0-0 ♗b7 8 ♖b1

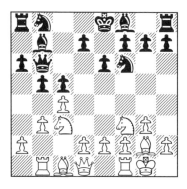

White cannot immediately continue with 8 ♗b2 because of 8...bxc4. White cannot then recapture on c4 with a pawn because doing so would expose the bishop to capture from the queen on b6. This looks like a concession to me already precipitated by my unusual but active set-up. White appears to be uncertain on where to deploy his central pawns. Their placements will influence heavily the conduct of the middlegame.

8...♗e7

I wanted to keep the option of playing the knight to c6 and playing ...d5 in one go so I developed the bishop first to prepare putting the king into safety by castling. Black's formation will resemble a Hedgehog after ...0-0, ...d6, ...♘bd7, and ...♖ac8.

9 e3 0-0 10 ♛e2 ♗c6

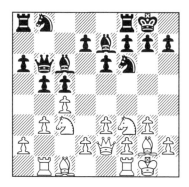

The increased pressure on b5 by the queen prompted me to respond with this strong bishop move. Black could also simply play 10...b4 and if White continues with 11 ♘a4, the queen can go to a7 with the idea of playing ...d6, ...♘bd7, ...♖ad8 and ♛a8.

11 ♗b2 d6

Covering e5 and preparing ...♘bd7.

12 ♖fd1 ♘bd7

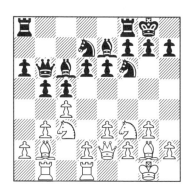

Both armies are fully developed. Now, it is time to consider the specifics of the middlegame plans. *The plan will come out of the pawn structures and piece placements. You cannot force a plan that is unnatural to your structure.*

This is one example of a game that will be decided less by avoidance of blunders or exploitation of blunders but more by strategic manoeuvring and exploitation of positional weaknesses, undeveloped pieces and scope-limited pieces. This is also where a knowledge and understanding of imbalances, as deftly explained and strongly espoused by IM Silman, will come in.

13 d4 ♛b7

It looks like Black has already equalized.

14 ♘e1

White plans d4-d5 but a better idea is 14 e4!? b4 15 ♘d5.

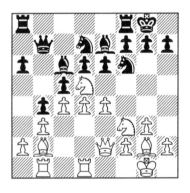

Elsewhere, I mentioned that moves placing minor or major pieces under threat of capture by a pawn are harder to see. This line should favour White.

14...♗xg2 15 ♘xg2 b4 16 ♘a4 ♘e4 17

f3 ♘g5?!

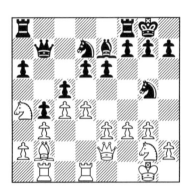

It is hardly ever good to move a piece to a square where it has no access to safety when attacked by an opponent's pawn. This means Black will waste a tempo in preventing the knight from being trapped. I thought I could buy the knight some time because of the threat on f3 but this idea was easily refuted by...

18 d5

By closing the diagonal White is threatening to trap the knight with h2-h4 next move.

18...♘h3+

This incursion is double-edged, but I needed to buy time in order to close the diagonal.

Giving the knight an escape square to h7 by 18...h6 was more prudent than sticking the knight into the lion's den. The return to f6 via h7 keeps the game still in balance.

19 ♔h1 e5 20 ♖f1 f5 21 e4

This move allows ...f4. Preferable for White is 21 f4 ♘f6 22 ♘e1 leaving him with an advantage.

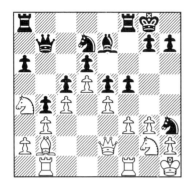

21...♖f7??

Black misses the opportunity to open the f-file with 21...f4. Once the file is opened, the f3-pawn would become weak and it would give Black a natural target to latch onto. Black would have an access route to the g- and h-files for his rooks. White was short on time and 21...f4 would have given Black practical winning chances and the initiative.

Having the initiative when your opponent is low on time adds a favourable element to the mix of imbalances. For example, here White would be forced to waste even more time figuring out a defensible set-up against the opening of the file. Time left on the clock before the time control plays an important role in overall strategy. *The possessor of the time advantage should strive to keep heavy pieces in play, especially the queen which has the most potent capability of exacting double attacks.* Double attacks occur often and are virtually always fatal in time trouble.

22 exf5 ♖xf5 23 ♘e3

This move wrests the initiative from Black and allows White to gain clock time, since Black has to calculate the consequences of where to post the rook. Meanwhile, the knight on h3 is feeling very uncomfortable. However, White has a better move in 23 f4! giving his queen access to the important g4-square.

23...♖ff8

The only good square. Black was wise to admit the wasted tempo and not submit to the beckoning arms of belligerence. I wanted so much to double rooks on the f-file but could not find a safe way of doing so without losing the knight on h3.

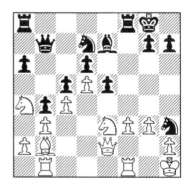

24 ♕g2??

White gives Black the chance to return into the game with no penalties for his knight's reckless intrusion into White's camp. He missed the strong 24 f4! with similar follow-up ideas involving ♕g4. This happens a lot in time trouble.

24...♘g5 25 f4

Finally, but it is not as effective as it

would have been one or two moves earlier.

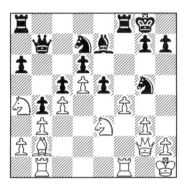

25...♘f7 26 ♖be1 ♘h6

I wanted to prevent White's knight from reaching g4 and adding pressure to my e5-pawn, but this is inaccurate. 26...♕c7!? is stronger. Black should keep the option of recapturing with a knight in case White takes on e5. A knight on e5 would be radiating power into White's camp.

27 fxe5 dxe5 28 ♕e4

A better move for White is 28 ♕h3 when Black has to be extra careful else the queen penetration on e6 can be fatal to his minor pieces. The safest course for Black is 28...♘f7 29 ♕e6 ♗f6, which keeps things under control but cedes a slight edge to White.

28...♗d6

Because of my inaccurate 26th move, the poor bishop is reduced to the unenviable role of a pawn. You should never demote a piece to such a role but here it was a positional necessity. On the bright side, besides defending e5 and c5, it doubles as a blockader on d6.

As a consolation, its counterpart on b2, if the cleric may have a say, is also unhappy though only momentarily. The sorry placements of the knight on a4 and the bishop on b2 gave me some hope for achieving equality if only I could swing both my rook and queen to the kingside. Without this imbalance, it would be reckless not to begin questioning the viability of my position.

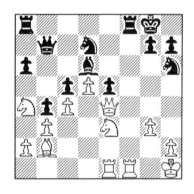

It is amazing how a positive outlook brought about by perceived tangibles can sometimes encourage the psyche to play on despite the objective truth on the board. I played like I had an extra piece even after demoting the bishop to its present role as a noble pawn defender.

28...♗f6 is probably a better try with the idea of bringing back the knight on h6 back to f7 and then to d6. In some lines, the knight on h6 will feel some discomfort from White's advancing g-pawn.

29 ♘f5

29 g4!? looks loose but it is a good move. Black's heavy pieces are not well

coordinated to take advantage of the courageous g-pawn. A pawn move in front of the castled king is not always bad especially when the opponent lacks the ability to exploit it or the un-defended squares it leaves behind (in this instance, the squares f4, h4, f3 and h3). If the advance serves an enabling function for the other pieces, then you can bravely take the chance.

29...♘xf5 30 ♖xf5

This recapture increases the pressure on the isolated pawn on e5.

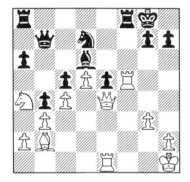

30...g6

I couldn't allow White to double rooks on the f-file and I needed to scare the rook away from the e-pawn even at the price of weakening the a1-h8 di-agonal. It was a good thing that the knight on a4 was too many moves away from pressuring e5 some more. If the pawn on e5 died, a queen and bishop battery along the diagonal would spell my quick doom. I avoided exchanging rooks on f5 because I thought the queen recapture would threaten ♕e6+ and win the bishop on

d6. My over-the-board analysis con-vinced me that preventing the check with ...♖ae8 would allow White to seize the f-file with his other rook and give him an even bigger edge. I also wanted to encourage White to take on f8 so I could relocate the a8-rook to the king-side with gain of tempo. The nudge did not work but it forced White to return the harassed rook to f1. Engine analysis later confirmed my fear with regards to the line 30...♖xf5 31 ♕xf5 ♖e8 as in-deed it would have given White a com-fortable edge.

31 ♖ff1 ♖ae8

I wanted to tempo the queen with the knight but I feared leaving the de-fence of the c-pawn solely to the over-worked bishop. Plus, I needed to pro-tect the weak e6-square from the queen. *Fritz* agrees with 31...♖ae8 but *Rybka* claims Black should first take on f1 intending to follow up with ...♖af8 to achieve near equality.

32 ♖xf8+ ♖xf8 33 ♕g4

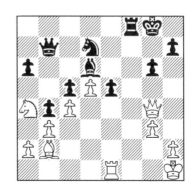

33...♖f5

After this move, I felt I could not lose

and would draw easily. White is slightly better according to the impartial chess engines but I evaluated the overall state of the game as better for me. Positivism or optimism as in life has a place in chess.

Arguing for my favour was the practical matter of being ahead on the clock. I cannot overemphasize the benefits of remaining strongly positive over your own chances during a struggle, but having an opponent who only has less than five minutes for seven moves is like being ahead by a pawn. *Positivism fuels energetic play and aptly reflects your move choices as they tend to be active rather than passive.* When the mind believes it is winning or just plain better, it tends to find sharper options. Negativism or pessimism, on the other hand, has a disabling effect to our game. Sulking over a lost position or the unexpected turn of events tends to fog the mind in finding resources.

Begin your search with the assumption that even in dire situations resources do exist. Stay positive. One effective way of doing so is to look for some redeeming points in your position. Identify and catalogue latent weaknesses or inactive pieces in the opponent's camp for exploitation either now or later. I know it is hard to do but not trying will make winning even harder. A more effective version of this routine involves mentally "verbalizing" the existing imbalances, both good and

bad, in both camps.

34 ♕e2

Anticipating ...♘f6, White decides to give up the attempt to occupy e6.

34...♕b8 35 ♖f1 ♕f8 36 ♔g2

36...♖xf1

An interesting try which my opponent pointed out during a short postmortem was 36...e4. My bias against opening the diagonal for a White battery blinded me to its mere possibility. I forgot that I had a dark-squared bishop ready to oppose the battery. The complications would have been to my favour as my opponent was dangerously low on time.

Because of their forcing nature, double exchanges on f1 gave my opponent easy moves to get closer to the time control. Time management in the world of increments or delays is part of the contest, so exploit it mercilessly. There is no dishonour in winning on time.

37 ♖xf1 37 ♕xf1 ♕xf1+

I could have tried 37...♕f5 38 ♕xf5 gxf5 39 a3 a5 reaching comfortable equality and with Black having one more pawn towards the centre.

38 ♔xf1 h5 39 ♗c1 ♔f7 40 ♔e2 ♔f6 41 ♗e3

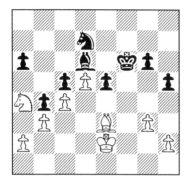

I do not see how Black can penetrate White's camp beyond the fourth rank. This time I waited for my esteemed opponent to make the draw offer because my earlier offer had been promptly refused without due consideration. It is not every day that a weaker player is in a situation where he can oppress his titled opponent with the discomfort of playing on with no other possible outcome for him but a draw.

41...g5 42 ♔f3 ♔f5 43 h3

43...g4+

Black can try 43...e4+ but White can simply play 44 ♔g2 with an easy draw.

44 hxg4+ hxg4+ 45 ♔f2 ♔e4 46 ♔e2 ♔f5 47 ♔f1 e4 48 ♔g2 ♔g6 ½-½

Draw agreed.

> ### Game 25
> **A.Hortillosa-J.Schuyler**
> Pawtucket 2008
> *English Opening*

1 c4

This was my third White of the tournament in five rounds. I wanted to improve my score as White so I chose to employ my main weapon for this tournament. I consider this to be my main weapon because it is the one opening set-up in my arsenal with which I received personal coaching from IM Mark Ginsburg, a well-known opening theorist.

One secret fear I had the whole time was what to do if my opponent would not cooperate and instead chose to answer with anything else but a King's Indian Defence. I really had no intention of playing the English but Black could elect to channel the game into that opening with 1...c5 or 1...e5.

1...g6 2 ♘c3 ♗g7 3 e4 c5

It took me a minute to realize I had fallen for a move-order trick. Black was now essentially playing the Hyper-Accelerated Dragon, one of my favourite set-ups against 1 e4. Due to an early c4, I could no longer play a quick d2-d4 because the d4-square was already attacked twice by Black and there's really no effective way of engineering the advance even with the preparatory ♘f3. Black could simply match the influence on d4 with ...♘c6 and if further necessary with ...e5. So I elected to play a set-up widely known as the Botvinnik system of the English Opening. Rogelio Barcenilla, a fellow émigré from the Philippines earned his third GM norm at the Copper State International in May 2009 employing this set-up more than once against strong opposition.

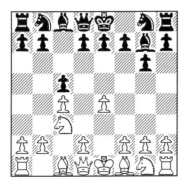

Black could also play 3...d6 aiming for a King's Indian, but this would have suited me just fine because I was itching to play against it anyway.

4 g3

I was tempted to play g2-g4, a move I have recently taken up with good results. However, the enormity and significance of the event dawned on me before I could get silly. But it took a lot of energy to restrain myself. An important tournament like this one is not the venue for experimentation or the forum to accrue experience with a new opening.

4...♘c6 5 ♗g2 e6 6 ♘ge2 ♘ge7

This reliable Black set-up has seen robust testing in countless master games.

In my annotations to my game against FM McIntyre, later in this book, I mention that ...e6 and ...♘ge7 make a natural pair in this particular set-up where you have a fianchettoed bishop on g7. The knight on e7 assists in the ...f5 and ...d5 breaks. In some lines, the knight on e7 redeploys to c6 with the idea of maintaining a knight on d4 after ...♘cd4 as an option.

7 0-0 0-0 8 d3

In the Closed Sicilian proper, I would now be playing ♗e3 gaining a tempo on the c5-pawn, but here I could not because I had yet to play d2-d3 to open the diagonal for the bishop. The benefit of having played c4 early is that Black cannot execute his ...d5 break without additional preparation in the present position.

8...a6 9 ♗g5

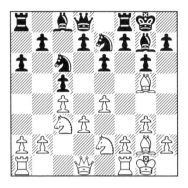

If 9 ♗e3 straightaway, Black can reply 9...d6. Or he can delay ...d6 and play instead 9...♘d4 10 ♗g5 h6 11 ♗d2 d6 12 ♘xd4 cxd4 13 ♘e2 e5 14 f4 ♕c7 with interesting play for both sides. My only reservation with 9...d6 is that it gives White the option to play 10 d4 taking control of the critical central square. The waste of tempo is justified in my mind because now the d4-square is off limits to Black's knight. Also, Black is not in the position to play ...cxd4. Amateur Sicilian players will almost always capture on d4 because that is what the brain is programmed to do in this line: the point of ...c5 is to exchange the less significant wing pawn for White's central pawn and open the c-file for Black as a route for counterplay. Here Black will likely not exchange on d4 because it will leave the d6-pawn backward. After ♕d2, White will be ahead in development and will have a ready-made plan of playing one of the rooks to d1 and exchanging off the bishop on g7 (with ♗h6).

9...h6 10 ♗e3

This looks like the natural square for the bishop. The controlling idea behind 10 ♗e3 was to form a battery with my queen with gain of tempo. But 10 ♗d2 is preferable. With the bishop on e3, White removes the option of exchanging knights on d4 because the recapture with a pawn will fork the knight on c3 and the bishop on e3.

10...♘d4

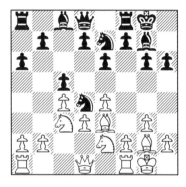

11 ♕d2

This move gains a tempo and induces Black to place his king on h7. In some lines it will become vulnerable to a bishop check on e4, and it also invites h2-h4-h5. You find these ideas in some of Fischer's games.

It is okay to borrow ideas in chess. In fact, it is highly encouraged. There is safety atop the shoulders of chess giants, past and present. There is no need to work out the details to check if the idea works. Playing over similar games and noting middlegame ideas in similar pawn structures and piece placements will save you study time. There are times and places in chess where originality is richly rewarded by the chess gods. But in most times, *familiarity of old ideas and alertness to its applicability in your own games will also win you points.*

11...♔h7

Another possibility is 11...h5.

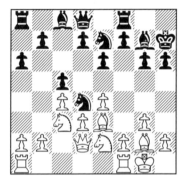

12 f4

White should consider playing on the queenside with 12 ♖ab1. I play this set-up as Black and I should have known better that the plan of f2-f4, ♖ff2 and ♖af1 would just end up wasting time because Black was ready to stop White's advance cold in one move with ...f5.

I remember reading somewhere that *before you expend tempi on a plan, first examine whether your opponent can stop the execution of a key move essential to the success of such a plan by using fewer moves than what it would take for you to reach the final preparation phase.* Many times we embark on a plan taking us three or even more moves to reach invasion point only to

be stopped cold just as we are about to execute the key move, by a single move from the opponent. Meanwhile, the opponent has spent the corresponding tempi on the other side of the board in preparation for his own plan and we suddenly find ourselves short of tempi to repulse his own invasion plan.

The reverse is true as well. Sometimes our opponent ignores our preparation plans either in the hope that we are wrong or that his own counterplay will arrive faster than ours. *Take the time to search for one move available to your opponent that has the force to effectively nullify the idea behind your plan.*

12...d6 13 ♖f2 ♖b8 14 ♖af1

Now White is one move away from playing f4-f5. I just needed to play one more preparatory move in g3-g4. But Black is alert to counter my optically nice-looking amassing of forces on the f-file.

14...f5

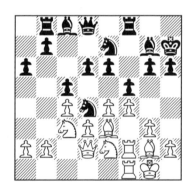

Did the ...f5 defensive move occur to Black just now by way of inspiration? I do not think so. He simply executed standard operating procedure against White's formation. Make a note: this is how Black should play against similar displays of aggression on White's part. Black will now have a free hand on the queenside. It is his turn to array his forces on the queenside and bring fear to White.

The informed player usually benefits from his stock chess knowledge, but the ignorant one succumbs to defeat. I have played games this way myself as Black, so why did I allow myself to get drawn to its false promises?

15 h3

This is why. I am resolute in my ambitions. I reached the point of no return where only the strong in heart deserves to fight for victory.

One might get tempted to play a2-a4 first with the idea of capturing on b5 twice, but that would only hasten Black's goal of opening invasion routes for his forces. Here a2-a4 weakens b3, and after ...b5 and ...bxc4 Black can harass the queen slowing down White's attack on the kingside while continuing his own. The player who gets distracted first ends holding the doughnut.

15...b5

Black has done the most he could do with ...f5 to slow White down. White was aptly aware that he could afford to attend to any distraction on the queenside. Each combatant was now committed to his own scheme of attack for ill or good.

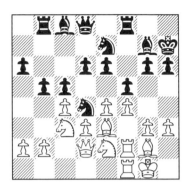

16 ♗xd4

My idea was to minimize Black's grip on f5 and to blunt the bishop's reach on b2. Interesting is 16 cxb5 axb5 17 b4 with even chances.

16...cxd4

After this move, my chess engines both pronounce Black as having a huge advantage.

17 ♘d1 bxc4

Not giving White the chance to shore up c4 with b2-b3. I had intended to redeploy the knight to b2 and to recapture on c4 with either the d-pawn or the knight.

18 dxc4 ♕b6 19 ♕d3 e5?

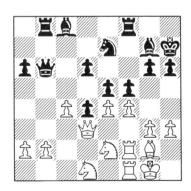

Black missed his chance in 19...fxe4 20 ♗xe4 d5 21 cxd5 exd5 22 ♗g2 ♗f5 23 ♕a3 ♖fe8 24 ♘c1 ♗e4 to obtain a huge advantage.

20 fxe5

This fitted my plan to open the f-file so I took the chance.

20...dxe5 21 g4?

This was a bluff and Black fell into it.

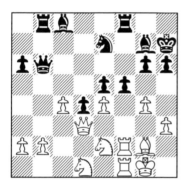

21...♘c6?

This is a gross error.

The counter-intuitive 21...f4 is best, after which Black has the lead. White's only counterplay is along the f-file and Black should have taken the opportunity to shut it down for good. Black is stronger on the queenside and it should be on this side of the board where he should be prospecting for gold.

I actually saw this possibility, but only after playing 21 g4. Play might continue as in 22 ♗f3 ♘c6 23 a3 a5 24 ♘c1 ♕c5 when Black is clearly better. It will be a miracle if White can hold this position.

Not grateful for the gift, I gave my opponent one last chance to correct his indifference to good fortune.

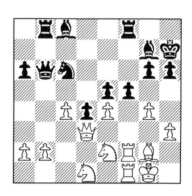

22 a3

Here I thought preventing the knight from reaching b4 was more important than allowing Black to shut down the f-file action. I intended to answer ...f4 with ♗f3 and then to transfer all my heavies to the queenside to support the advance of my queenside majority. I overlooked that Black had to recapture on f5 first after exf5 before he could play ...♘b4 as the queen could simply ignore the threat because White could take on g6 with check – winning a pawn.

22 exf5 must be played now before Black notices the ...f4 idea: 22...gxf5 23 ♘g3 ♘b4 24 ♕b3 f4 with equal chances.

22...♗f6?

Black has made two bad moves in a row, and the game is now better for White. I never understood the point behind this move, even now. Both chess engines point to this error as the straw that broke the camel's back.

23 exf5

White could not forego this opportunity any longer. Black has one last move in ...♗b7 before he starts looking around for something like ...f4. The right capture, and the engines agree with me.

23...gxf5

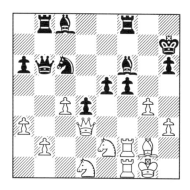

24 gxf5

24 ♘g3 is better than what I played. I was afraid of 24...e4 due to some faulty analysis. It was only after I made the move that I realized I could simply take the pawn with the knight. The game may continue 25 ♘xe4 fxe4 26 ♕xe4+ ♔g7 27 ♕xc6 ♕xc6 28 ♗xc6 and White should be okay. He is two pawns up and Black's passed d-pawn is going nowhere.

24...♖g8 25 ♔h1 ♗b7

Despite White's pawn advantage, Black has an active position and is to be preferred. My knights are poorly placed and will take time for meaningful redeployment. But there is hope because there is some iota of counterplay along the open g-file. Besides, the pawns on the queenside and the passed f-pawn have a menacing look to them and could worry Black. These are, of course, defanged but the pseudo threats can potentially busy Black with nonexistent dangers.

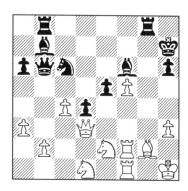

I noticed my opponent looking forlorn at this point so I began to act with confidence hoping that my demeanour would help confirm his fears.

26 ♘g3 ♘d8

He wants to go f7 and then d6 to help in getting his pawn rollers moving.

27 ♗xb7 ♕xb7+ 28 ♘e4 ♘f7 29 ♔h2

This gets out of the pin and tempos the bishop on f6. Suddenly, White is looking active.

29...♗g5

I did not like this move for Black because it allowed me to challenge the g-file without conceding anything. Black could have just defended the bishop with 29...♕c6.

30 ♖g1

I looked at 30 c5 briefly. With a6 unprotected, Black would not be able to play his next move, which proved to be a little annoying. Both players were running very low on time and direct threats were beginning to influence the course of the game.

30...♕b3 31 ♕f1

I kept the queens on because he was down to less than a minute whereas I had over five.

31...♗f4+

32 ♖xf4

Played instantly.

32...exf4 33 ♖xg8

My opponent was down to seconds when I played the move. I was afraid to leave the g3-square unprotected and was ready to give up my time advantage just to figure out the consequences. We both had seven moves to make to reach the first time control.

33 ♘f6+ is more precise than what I played, but as a practical matter keeping the knight on the board was useful because it gave me mating chances. Play may continue 33...♔h8 34 ♘xg8 ♖xg8 35 ♖xg8+ ♔xg8 and Black gets to continue in the fight.

33...♔xg8 34 ♕xf4

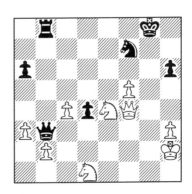

My opponent was hanging by a thread on his clock, down to meagre seconds. I am sure he was thankful for the 5-second delay.

34...♖c8 35 ♕g4+

This move has some very nasty intentions.

35...♔f8

Black chooses the wrong square in time pressure, and now he is lost.

He should have gone to the corner with 35...♔h8. But the quick reaction from the mind is to avoid scary-looking corners where mates do usually occur, especially when taken in the context of the looming f5-f6. The eventual ill fate of the black king provides another compelling argument for vigilance in confronting biases in chess thinking with concrete chess moves. *Sometimes hunches are not enough where brute calculations of variations are necessary to arrive at the truth.*

36 f6

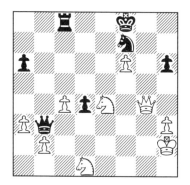

This was the best move of the game. It allows the possible check on g7 and seals the escape square on e7 not to mention the fatal discovered attack on the rook on c8.

36...♛xc4

Black protects the rook on c8 with this queen capture but at the price of the dear lady's own life. The delay had kept my opponent from overstepping the time control but he was down to around 10 seconds when he played the move. I was now down to less than a minute myself. In my haste, I transposed the winning move sequence.

37 ♘d6

The devastating check first via 37

♛g7+ ♚e8 and only then 38 ♘d6+ would have won the queen next move. *In ordering the sequence of your candidate moves, always consider first the most forcing one.*

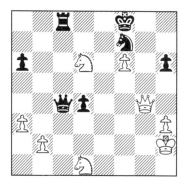

37...♛c2+ 38 ♚g1

Even better is 38 ♚g3 but in time trouble all wins are the same.

38...♛xd1+

To avoid losing on time, the lady gives up her life to gift the king a few further seconds to live.

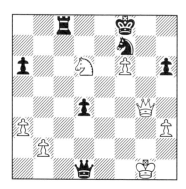

I was not expecting Black to give up the queen on d1 and my hand simply executed my intended 39 ♛g7 "mate", not realizing that now because of the capture I was in check. My opponent stopped the clock and claimed "illegal move". The TD had to verify the penalty and dutifully added time to his clock as a guilt offering. Because of the touch-move rule, I was forced to move the queen by which time the obvious became clear to my opponent.

39 ♕xd1 ♘xd6 40 ♕xd4 1-0

Realizing the hopelessness of his position, he resigned. Scoring three points in five rounds and not seeing a loss in four consecutive rounds against this level of opposition was a new experience for me. I began to imagine better possibilities ahead.

Sadly, I would lose in the next four rounds. In this tournament I learned an important lesson about stamina. You have got to be in shape to fare well in these 9-round events. *Even your sleeping and eating habits must be in good order.* Otherwise you will find yourself severely exhausted by the second half when good physical form matters most.

Game 26
A.Hortillosa-R.Hungaski
Pawtucket 2008
Torre Attack

This seventh-round game was the second game of the day. In the morning round, I had lost to IM Sarkar. It is hard to prepare for the day's second-round opponent in a Swiss format. You only know who you will be playing against in the morning round so preparation is focused on that particular opponent. Most of my preparation for the day was directed towards my game against Sarkar. Preparation gets harder still when you lose the day's first-round game for obvious reasons. Meeting two strong IMs on the same day was too much even for the "lucky" ones.

I eventually settled for 1 ♘f3 hoping to transpose to the Torre Attack based on a token preparation just before the round started. I noticed that my opponent plays 1...♘f6 most of the time against 1 ♘f3 and continues with ...e6 if White plays d2-d4 on move two. That was the extent and depth of my preparation. I strictly relied on my stock but old knowledge of the opening set-up for this encounter. As you will see later, my scant preparation was almost enough to secure at least a draw.

1 ♘f3 ♘f6 2 d4 e6

White players who wish to play the Torre Attack get irrationally excited when this position appears on the board. I must confess I did too.

The Torre Attack proper is normally reached via the move order 1 d4 ♘f6 2 ♘f3 e6 3 ♗g5. So why did I open with 1 ♘f3 if wanted to play the Torre after all? The answer is simple: I wanted to reach the Torre Attack formation via a move-order trick in a way that avoids other popular defences to 1 d4.

Experienced Torre Attack players know that when Black plays ...d5 on move two, White cannot enforce the Torre set-up without Black's cooperation. Why? Because after 1 d4 ♘f6 2 ♘f3 d5 3 ♗g5, Black has the annoying 3...♘e4, an option available to him courtesy of the move order he has chosen. White players feel cheated when Black gets this opportunity.

White players who are given to imposing their intention came up with a rather cunning move order, which effectively removes this option off the plate. Before I give you the move order, let me digress a little bit. A few years back I started experimenting with 3 c3 after 2...d5 and would patiently wait for Black's response. By the way, my move would usually get a head shake and a smile. But in quite a few games, Black would continue with 3...e6 and I would happily trot out 4 ♗g5 when the ...♘e4 move is no longer possible. Meanwhile, I would feel very smart indeed in tricking Black into allowing my favourite Torre while removing his other effective set-ups such as the

Hedgehog or a similar set-up involving a double fianchetto and playing ...d6 to cover the e5-square, rendering the standard invasion point inhabitable to White's knight.

The move order I was alluding to above begins by playing a Trompowsky as in 1 d4 ♘f6 2 ♗g5, and after 2...e6 3 ♘f3 White gets the standard Torre position he prefers. Black can still insist on playing on move two the annoying ...♘e4 and continuing with ...d5, but only players who are not averse to playing against the Tromp would venture into this path. On scant occasions where Black gets into this scheme the White player must be willing to play the Tromp or the trickster falls victim to a counter move-order trick.

3 ♗g5 h6

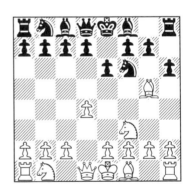

This is the move I also prefer to play against the Torre. Black wants to gain the bishop pair in exchange for a delay in development. A fair trade if you ask anybody who plays both sides. Sometimes I retreat to h4 maintaining the pin and then work to transpose the

game into a Queen's Gambit Declined. Most times, I capture the knight on f6 as in this game.

Having those options available to you is an artificial yet efficient way, given the constraints common to amateurs, of building a somewhat broader repertoire. Practically speaking, that is how you broaden your repertoire. Look at two or three lines you like playing with and then collapse the diverging points to a common move as the branching point of your repertoire. This way, you will not be so predictable.

4 ♗xf6 ♕xf6

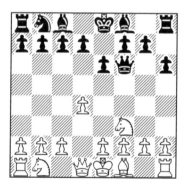

5 e4

Of course White has other possibilities which are equally good. I chose the central duo because it tends to limit the scope of one of the bishops depending on Black's chosen set-up. Black's opening set-up is based on the inherent advantages of the bishop pair. His middlegame plan, therefore, is one that emphasizes the power of the bishop pair. White, for his part, cannot allow Black to have open lines for the

bishops so the threat of advancing the e-pawn to e5 nudges Black to capitulate into shutting in his dark-squared bishop with ...d6.

5...d6 6 ♘c3

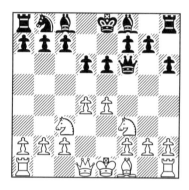

White, having the lead in development, must hurry to complete it so he can begin his campaign of aggression before Black can secure his king.

Opening set-ups are really a clash of chess ideas or chess beliefs. Here, White believes his lead in development will amount to something before Black can reorganize his counterplay in a manner that showcases the inherent advantage possessed in the bishop pair. Lately, however, I began to question White's propositional assumption. If most ways of transforming a lead in development into a winning advantage involve the opening of lines into Black's camp, doesn't that also benefit Black? This notion is easily falsified if we can demonstrate a way for White to open lines but only those which he can gainfully exploit for his advantage. Is it possible in most pawn structure configurations to open lines for White but still keep Black's bishop pair shut in? I guess the answer to that should become White's middlegame plans. So, there you have it. Your middlegame plans should arise from the answers to some questions regarding imbalances specific to pawn structures, yours and your opponent's. *The key is coming up with the right questions.*

Note that it is a rational possibility to find the right answers to the wrong questions. Your search for answers will yield answers but the plans will be wrong-headed because the answers, while correct, do not fit the pawn structures and the dynamic imbalances on the board. It sounds incongruous for someone like me who touts a blunder-proof chess thinking process to say that in the struggle to achieve lasting chess improvement, tactical proficiency alone will come to naught. *Tactical proficiency can only take you to some height you have never reached before but it will leave you stranded hopeless against strong and enlightened players.* For many chess lovers, just getting to a new height has become the journey itself. Being stranded atop any height is no fun because, being stranded, you are still able to go nowhere. I challenge you to aspire for more and to scale even greater heights. If I could do it, you can too.

6...a6 7 ♕d2

White is ready to castle queenside. I delayed developing the bishop because I wasn't sure where it should be. Since I was certain about castling queenside, I proceeded to do just that first.

7...g5

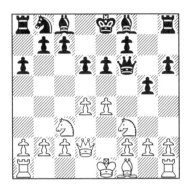

I felt some uneasiness about this move because it was obvious my d-pawn would come under pressure once the bishop got to g7. I could not understand the point of ...a6, but once we got here it came to me. Black will add pressure to the d-pawn by way of ...♘c6 but with b5 inaccessible to my bishop, I have to find other means to secure its life from harm. Even more serious is the threat of ...g4, forcing the knight to move away from the defence of the d-pawn.

Black has succeeded in slowing White from completing his development. The remarkable thing is that he did it all with just pawn moves. I got very suspicious here. I just could not believe this was even a possibility for Black. For my response, I thought I had to protect the f4-square with a pawn to prevent the exchange of queens after White castles long (with ...♕f4) and also to anticipate posting the knight on h4 if attacked by ...g4. I also noticed that g2-g3 right away loses a piece since the knight on f3 hangs. Eventually I settled for something non-committal in h2-h3, which is intended to discourage Black from pushing his g-pawn because then it would open the h-file for my rook.

8 h3 ♗g7 9 ♗e2

I regretted posting the bishop on e2 a few moves later. My hand felt it really should belong on c4 but I had an aversion to the exchange of queens, for without my queen the ferocity of my attack would be severely diminished. Without the queens on board, the bishop pair would yield Black tangible advantages. Come to think about it now, shouldn't that be a concern for White? Granting the power of the bishop pair, should I be the one aiming for the queen exchange to blunt the wielding of such power?

9...♘c6 10 0-0-0

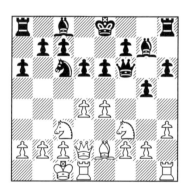

If this is not a picture of being ahead in development, what is?

10...♗d7

Black until now has managed to keep his castling ambition hidden. The position allows him to castle either side. Will he go for opposite castling so we could bludgeon each other to death or will he go for a fight in the middle?

11 ♔b1

Instead of the text, I should have gone for 11 e5. I thought I had time for it. The motivation behind 11 ♔b1 was to disallow the exchange of queens. But seeing that Black is running out of constructive moves besides castling, I could have ventured with 11 e5 since it is best played while Black is uncastled.

11...0-0-0

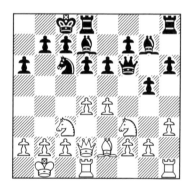

After this, I felt that Black had caught up in development while I had lost some advantage. But I got over it and quickly realized that the time to determine the specifics of a middle-game plan had arrived.

12 ♖he1

Centralizing a rook cannot be wrong so I did it without much thought.

12...♖hg8 13 ♗c4

Since I never got to play g2-g3, defending the knight with ♗e2 turned out to be a wasted tempo. If the bishop was already on c4, White could now play 13 ♕d3 with dangerous threats.

13...h5

I do not know why I didn't expect this move, as there is obviously a dearth of possibilities on the board except along the h-file. I had planned to play ♕e2 as follow up to ♗c4 with the idea of threatening to sacrifice my cleric for two pawns on a6 but after 13...h5, the simple ...g5-g4 could potentially spoil White's fleeting fun.

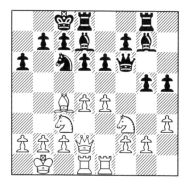

14 ♕e3

It is time to look at imbalances. Material is equal but Black's bishop on d7 is underperforming. White's centre is maintainable and there are no serious weaknesses in both camps. Both kings are relatively safe. Black may have a slight advantage on the kingside because he can forcibly open the h-file at will. The principal idea of the text move was to provide extra support to the e-

pawn so I could meet ...g5-g4 with e4-e5. But I hated losing the initiative to Black albeit temporarily.

This surely was one of the critical junctures in the game. The wise thing to do here is to ascertain the soundness of my interrelated ideas by brute force calculations. I remember getting excited about White's chances around this point despite the slight irritation posed by ...g4. The immediate threat against the steed with ...g4, and the imminent threat to my queen if placed on e2 to form a battery along the f1-a6 diagonal nudged me to abandon the sacrificial sortie on a6 momentarily. I did not calculate actual variations, which was to my downfall, but the attraction to the idea was undeniably strong.

It took me a long time to figure out a way of protecting my d-pawn if one of its defenders – the knight on f3 – was driven away by ...g4 and at the same time retaining the option of sacrificing the bishop on a6 and recapturing with the queen with check. For the plan to work, a number of things must first be true:

1. The a1-h8 diagonal must be closed.

2. The queen must be able to get to a6 with check.

3. A rook penetration into the queenside must be feasible via a rook-lift to aid the queen in a mating attack.

With all these conditions in mind, I arrived at the candidate move: 14 ♕e3.

14...g4

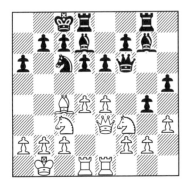

15 e5

So, here we go. How will Black continue? Black took over 20 minutes on his next move. I had spent over 22 minutes on 14 ♕e3.

15...♕h6

I expected this move so my response was immediate, one second to be exact according to my MonRoi PCM. Instead, 15...♕g6 16 ♘h4 ♕h6 17 hxg4 ♕xe3 18 fxe3 dxe5 19 gxh5 exd4 20 exd4 ♗xd4 21 ♗e2 gives Black a slight advantage. Just so you know I did not get this far in my calculations. It was not necessary because I did not like the idea at first glance. A lackadaisical attitude, but it is hard to avoid being lazy sometimes.

16 ♘g5

I am happy to see my judgment of the position confirmed by chess engines. Both beasts confirm White has achieved equality after this move. This simple fact breeds confidence in one's abilities. *It is sensible to be aware of one's limitations and foolhardy to ignore them but in my mind it is equally calamitous to play with plenty of dis-*

trust. That's right. Play like you are their equal and the brain may even surprise you.

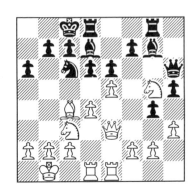

16...d5

My esteemed opponent, who never showed any signs of discomfort on his face with regards to what was happening on the board, took almost 12 minutes and calmly executed his move. Since he had spent over 30 minutes for his last two moves, I began to feel better about my position. What was he worried about I asked? Instead of wasting time solving the puzzle of his concern, I should have checked for flaws in my calculations.

17 ♗xa6??

This was the initial salvo of a flawed plan. The emotional investment on this move started to accrue on move 13, but Black's attack against the knight on f3 threw a spanner in the works. The change in pawn structure and the closing of the a1-h8 diagonal are recent events with big enough tremors on the landscape providing White with cues to change plans.

This happens when one falls prey to the escalation of commitment fallacy. Because of the sunk cost already wasted on the plan, I was unwilling to simply let it go as necessary losses. This happens a lot in the business world as well. The prudent action is to change course and to carry the expended resources as loss. But I tried hard to justify the plan I felt was wrong-headed. *Often in chess the wisest course is to acknowledge a bad plan as such, abort the plan, erase it from memory and change course.*

I had planned on sacrificing the bishop for the pawn on a6 followed by ♕e2. I also thought that Black would not allow a queen check on a6, which would give me time to capture on f7 and win the exchange. Two pawns and a rook, I thought, were good compensation for the two minor pieces. I also saw the possibility of moving the c3-knight somewhere and playing ♖d3 intending to shuttle it to the a- or b-file to help the queen attack the slightly exposed black king.

Either the bishop retreat to b3 or d3 is much better than losing its life in a suicidal mission. I actually considered the moves 17 ♗d3 and 17 ♗f1 during my think and wondered how Black would continue.

17...bxa6 18 ♕e2

18...♘b8?!

Ignoring the a-pawn and simply grabbing the knight on g5 would have given Black the advantage. The position may look scary for Black, but two pieces for two pawns is more than a comfortable exchange. On top of the loot, the Black monarch can be easily protected by the minors, which provides an impregnable wall around it. After 18...♕xg5 19 ♕xa6+ ♔b8 20 ♘b5 ♕e7 21 ♖e3, White has no compensation for the sacrificed materials.

This was the position I was aiming for when I got carried away by the flawed decision to unnecessarily complicate matters with 17 ♗xa6. Who would not get excited over this dream position? I guess, only the fearless and you might add the foolish. No doubt, the latter aptly describes my brashness. I just hope my opponent didn't feel insulted with my unrestrained conduct. After all, I was playing against an IM with a FIDE rating of 2407.

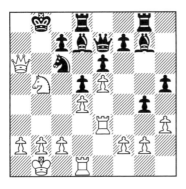

Looking deeper it turned out Black could simply cash in by giving back one piece with the pragmatic 17...♗c8 18 ♕xc6 ♗b7 and still keep a winning advantage. I reckon the menacing presence of the rook on the third rank ready to swing into action deterred Black from going into the variation. Once again brute force calculation is necessary to trump unfounded fears.

19 ♘xf7

This was my bailout plan in case Black felt insecure and rebuffed the knight sacrifice on g5. It is funny that the chess engines actually grant me the advantage with this line, rather than with the line that I wish I had gotten. The latter was the by-product of my optimistic evaluation of the resulting position while the former was based more on the existential reality of the board. Machines are hardly swayed by

optimism; only positive raw numbers matter.

19...♕g6 20 ♘xd8 ♖xd8 21 hxg4

The decision to take on g4 was easy as it creates a vulnerable pawn no matter how Black recaptures.

21...hxg4

I evaluated this position to be better for White and both engines are in agreement with me.

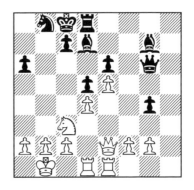

22 ♖d3

My original plan involved attacking the black king directly via the open b-file. But when the position on the kingside clarified, my attention was drawn to the vulnerable g-pawn. While I was not sure then if I would succeed in winning it, I was fully convinced that its demise would lead to a big advantage due to the resulting passed g-pawn. My rooks would also realize their full potential behind the advancing pawns. Then I hit on the idea of combining both threats. To feint an attack against the king starting with this rook-lift from d1 to d3 looked brilliant. My real target was the pawn on g4.

I showered myself with generous credit for pausing the plan tempo long enough to realize the drastic change in the structure. It sounds self-serving and pretentious but it is one skill set I labour to possess especially at those critical junctures. But to be honest, the switch in plans was motivated primarily by my inability to figure out a faster way of bringing attacking pieces to bear on the compromised position of the black king. The big plus about the rook-lift is the added convenience it provides in keeping the option of attacking the king.

It was only while analyzing this game for the book that I saw a better way of threatening the g-pawn using the other rook via 22 ♖h1 and ♖h4. It turns out that Black has some defensive resources as the following line shows: 22 ♖h1 ♖f8 23 ♖h4 ♖f4 24 g3 ♖f3 25 ♖d3 c5 26 dxc5 ♕f5 27 ♖xf3 gxf3 28 ♕d3 ♕xe5 29 ♕xf3 ♕e1+ 30 ♘d1 ♘c6 31 ♖h1 ♘d4 32 ♖xe1 ♘xf3 33 ♖h1 when White still has to work to win. But the burden to find these resources squarely rests on Black's shoulders and it's not easy. Again the idea of giving your opponent problems to solve not only increases the likelihood for errors to creep in to his play but it also heightens his feeling of danger, which can be harmful to his overall emotional state. *Distress on the board callously disturbs the equilibrium of the mind and often with irreparable damage.*

22...♖f8

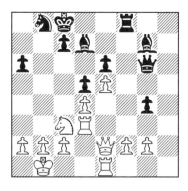

My opponent saw my plan and came up with this active defensive set-up. I must admit I failed to consider Black's possible reaction to my plan.

During critical points of the game, you should take the time to falsify your own plan. The point is to find defensive schemes by your opponent that will nullify your threats. Had I done this, I would for sure have realized that I would lose a tempo to defend d4 if Black actively defended g4 with ...♖f4. Seeing this possibility would have prompted me to search for another way of attacking g4 while keeping d4 defended. This reconnaissance data would have pointed me to the rook on e1 as the suitable attacker and not the rook on d1. Attacking the g-pawn from the flank on h4 would discourage Black from defending it with ...♖f4 because I could simply play g2-g3 and the rook is driven away. This means the right move was 22 ♖h1 to be followed by ♖h4.

23 ♖g3

Interesting is 23 ♖h1!? ♗h6 24 f3,

with White holding some advantage.

23...♖f4

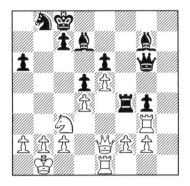

Now Black threatens the d-pawn and White must waste a tempo to protect it from capture. At this point the chess engines change their evaluation to equal.

24 ♖d1

This move was clearly the obvious choice given the demands of the position, yet making it was hard to do. It felt like I just lost the game right here.

I do not know why there are so few writings on the influence, either good or bad, of the state of the psyche during a chess game. There might be some empirical work on it but it has not reached popular saturation because I cannot recall reading one. The game is evaluated as equal by chess engines because that is the reality in its mathematical construct, yet in the mind of at least one player Black has just turned the tables. My opponent was now playing with newfound enthusiasm. I suspect he now believed that he was much better.

It is amazing how one's decisive play can sometimes elicit the opposite response across the other side. It seems like we get easily affected mentally by the demeanour of our opponents. It is known that when Kasparov overtly shows disdain over his opponent's move by way of body language, the suggestive nature of this somehow becomes a reality in his opponent's play. It goes like this: when Kasparov frowns on your move as one having the mark of a patzer, your successive play becomes what we jokingly describe as that of a "patzer".

24...c5

25 dxc5

25 ♕e3 doesn't help because of 25...♕f5 26 f3 cxd4 27 ♖xd4 ♖xd4 28 ♕xd4 ♘c6 when White cannot avoid losing the e-pawn.

25...♕f5 26 f3 gxf3 27 gxf3 ♗xe5

Both chess engines still agree that the position remains equal even after the loss of the pawn. Remember: they only speak the language of reality unencumbered by emotion. *The reversal of fortune, whether real or not, is emotionally burdensome to the player who lost it.* Here, I began to fear Black's d- and e-pawns.

28 ♖g8+?

This is an inexplicable positional blunder that surrenders the advantage to Black. The rook should have never left the defence of f3. With the rook still on g3 protecting f3, White can then continue as in the game by giving up the knight for the passed d- and e-pawns. If the black rook takes on f3, the white rook recaptures thereby eliminating the back rank mate threat. White will then restore the material balance by capturing the pinned bishop on e5.

The right sequence is 28 ♘xd5 exd5 29 ♖xd5 ♖d4. Black's last move is a clever one, and this is the only way for him to keep the balance. White cannot yet take on e5 because of the bank rank mate on d1 but he could after 30 ♖g8+ ♔b7 31 ♖xb8+ ♔xb8 32 ♖xe5. I cannot imagine Black not accepting a draw here.

28...♔b7 29 ♘xd5??

Reckless aggression, I would say. But the idea had merit had the rook not strayed from g3.

29...exd5 30 ♖xd5 ♖xf3

It is amazing how move sequences in chess can sway evaluations from draw to loss or win in an instant. Now the tactical continuation 31 ♖xb8+ ♔xb8 32 ♕xe5 ♕xe5 33 ♖xe5 no longer works because of the bank rank mate with ...♖f1. In this line, the loss of the f-pawn is fatally consequential because it gives Black access to White's compromised back rank.

31 ♖g1 ♖f2 32 ♕xe5?? 0-1

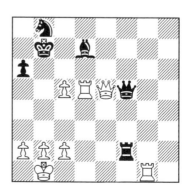

I had seen the bank rank mate motif and protected against it by 31 ♖g1 but somehow I forgot it after 31...♖f2. I resigned before Black could make his move. You can only imagine my disappointment! Halving the point with the IM would surely have emboldened me for the last two rounds.

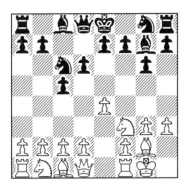

> *Game 27*
> **P.MacIntyre-A.Hortillosa**
> Pawtucket 2008
> *Sicilian Defence*

With this being the last round of the tournament and having lost the morning round, my only goal was to draw so I could get my initial rating over 2200 FIDE. Finishing with 3½ points out of 9 would exceed my initial goal of 1 point by a margin.

1 e4 c5 2 ♘f3 g6 3 g3 ♗g7 4 ♗g2 d6 5 0-0 ♘c6 6 h3

White elects to deviate from book lines with this move. The choice, however, is a bit slow and allows Black to develop comfortably.

6...e6

6...e5 is one other line I often use as Black against White's fianchetto set-up. White has two good continuations in either 7 c3 or 7 d3. Black can expect reasonable middlegame chances against either set-up with 7...♘ge7.

7 c3 ♘f6

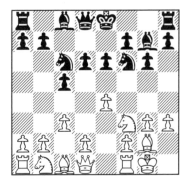

I normally do not continue with ...♘f6, especially when ...e6, has been played. Looking at this game one week later, I could not remember what I was afraid of that led me to post the knight on f6 instead of following generally established wisdom, which dictates playing it to e7. I was probably mixing systems here, a known defect in amateur play. When ...e6 is played, Black normally should follow through with ...♘ge7. These two moves are a natural pair.

Most strong players including the late world champion Botvinnik would prefer ...♘e7 even with the pawn on e5. The advantage of posting it on e7 is that the natural break ...f7-f5 is ready to go whereas in the position where the knight is on f6, Black has to waste a tempo before he can play ...f5. Also, if White beats Black to playing f5 first (after f2-f4), Black may want to capture twice on f5: first with ...exf5 and second with a piece, but not with the g-pawn because it weakens the structure around the king. Black cannot afford in most cases to have a white pawn sitting on f5. A pawn on f5 means Black must always be on guard against the advance f6 forking the knight on e7 and the bishop on g7. In some Grand Prix Attack lines, the thematic advance from f5 to f6 creates tactical opportunities for the first player.

One data point on the board that rules out ...♘f6 in favour of ...♘e7 is White's h2-h3. Without the pawn advance, the knight can harass the dark-squared bishop when it reaches e3 with the manoeuvre ...♘g4. Here, it is no longer possible. I think the only motivation I had for choosing ...♘f6 over ...♘e7 was to gain a tempo and to induce White to misplace the rook. Since the move c2-c3 signals White's intention of playing for the centre with d2-d4, a direct attack against the e-pawn would preclude the defence with d2-d3. I wanted White to move the rook off the f-file to slow down the standard f2-f4-f5 advance typical of a Closed Sicilian formation.

I am not sure now if my provocation only helped White. Who profits with the rook on e1 is not clear based on my current understanding of positional play at this stage of my chess development. I am hopeful that a more mature understanding of strategic or positional play will come to me over time. I am fully aware despite my strong emphasis on tactics in my writing that correctly judging a position is another aspect of over-the-board chess, which needs to be further developed if one wishes to reach master level.

8 ♖e1 0-0 9 d4

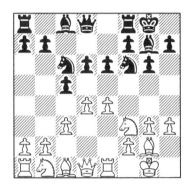

9...♕c7

Here I thought of responding with 9...e5 instead of the text move but my aversion to "wasting" a tempo, having moved the e-pawn already once, ruled supreme. However, one is not served well if past data is brought into the move selection process. *A far more efficient move selection process is one that limits the data set to the present position.* It is clear that our human biases are our undoing on many occasions.

In one of our email exchanges during the writing of this book, John Emms brought to my attention an example where theory has recognized this kind of tempo loss as in this line: 1 e4 c5 2 ♘f3 e6 3 d3 ♘c6 4 g3 g6 5 ♗g2 ♗g7 6 0-0 ♘ge7 7 ♖e1 d6 8 c3, where Black's best move is known to be 8...e5! How many times do we see a grandmaster move the same piece in succession as a reaction to the opponent's move? While this baffles the amateurs to no end, it makes perfect sense to master class players.

The algorithm routines of chess engines, from what little I know, do not bring into the equation where the pieces or pawns stood previously. It computes more than it searches for candidate moves based solely on where the pieces or pawns are standing now as the starting point of its search algorithm. It is totally indifferent to where these pieces used to be. That's why a chess engine is not only efficient but precise as well in its calculation of variations because its thinking process, as we call it in human terms, is simply not occluded by non-existing data sets. *We are best served if we strive to emulate the chess engines in this regard.*

While humans benefit from memory markers, machines have no relevant use for them. In fact, *most of our computational errors are due to presumptions stored in our memory.* You may recall from your experience these familiar words: "Oh no, I thought the king could not go there because my bishop was controlling the diagonal." We have forgotten that the bishop would be traded two moves later into the combinational sequence. Our failing rested on one flaw: former facts were still treated as real data sets in our computations. We fall victim to these residual memory markers too often.

Humans unlike machines cannot ignore previous moves. This best explains our tendency to miss strong retreating moves. My point becomes clear by using this scenario example. When a strong player is shown a position and is asked to find the best continuation, he sometimes suggests moving a piece or pawn that has only just moved. I have seen numerous cases of strong players suggesting moving a piece back to where it was a few moves earlier. An even more empathic example is one where a strong player suggests moving a piece back to where it was only one move ago. This occurs because he did not know the game history and was unburdened by the bias of the past; he simply made the choice based on the demands of the current position.

We can also place part of the blame on our strong bias for rules like the one strongly etched in our chess minds dictating the avoidance of wasting a tempo. What could be more tempo-wasting than moving the same piece back to where it was one move ago? A possible fix is to not allow knowledge of temporal facts, as in the bishop on c4 used to be on f1 so I cannot move it back to f1, to influence our search for candidate moves. The solution to our bias for rules is to turn the positive rule on its head by asking the simple query: why not? For the rule that says, "Capture towards the centre," we should ask, "Why not capture away from the centre?"

Returning to the position in the game, there's one further question: Why not exchange on d4? Isn't that what Black normally plays in the Sicilian? When White has played c2-c3, as a general rule Black should avoid exchanging his c-pawn for the d-pawn on d4 because here White has the option of recapturing with the c-pawn thereby obtaining a strong pawn centre duo. In other Sicilian lines when d2-d4 is played early, White does not have this option available to him. Also, once the c3-pawn recaptures and the square now vacated, the white knight will be able to get to its natural square in one move. Keeping the tension forces White to find another way of developing the queen's knight. If given the choice, White would rather develop the queen's bishop before the queen's knight but the position does not yet provide a good square for the bishop. If it goes to g5, Black can challenge it with ...h7-h6. When challenged, it can only retreat to f4 or d2 but not e3 because the e-pawn hangs. On f4, Black can gain time again by attacking it with ...♘h5, which also facilitates the natural break ...f5.

10 a4

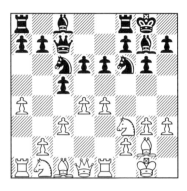

The only logical choice left for developing the queen's knight without blocking the bishop is the text move, planning ♘a3, but this hardly threatens Black so he is free to continue his development. The question is how best to continue my set-up. I ruled out playing ...h7-h6 because it is a far more useful move if the bishop is already on g5.

10...a6

Preventing ♘b5 (after ♘a3) and preparing my break on the queenside with ...b7-b5. Reflecting on it now, the better move is to develop the bishop or transfer the rook to d8. Allowing ♘b5 is not too bad because it will only make the ...b5 break develop even faster after ...a7-a6. Also, if the knight is on b5, it can only retreat to the ugly square on a3. Removing this option from White leads him to play it to c4 where it cannot be dislodged without due preparation.

11 ♘a3 ♖b8

11...cxd4 12 cxd4 d5 13 e5 ♘e4 is an interesting alternative, even though the bishop on c8 is hemmed in. The presence of dynamic imbalances on the board guarantees play for both sides.

12 dxc5 dxc5 13 ♘c4

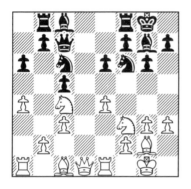

When I played 11...♖b8, I intended to continue with 13...b5 but noticed during reconnaissance that White had the possibility of 14 ♗f4 with really nasty intentions. I thought of playing 13...e5 now to render f4 inaccessible to the bishop but I was afraid of giving up the d5-square for the knight on c4 via e3. Black can dream of a set-up involving a pawn on h6, a bishop on e6 and a rook on d8. I would not mind meeting anyone as Black with this set-up. By anyone, I meant players below 2400.

13...♘e8

Besides wasting a critical tempo, this move also creates a latent threat to my rook on f8. It is very unsafe to box in a major piece like a rook especially when a pawn is not available to blunt a diagonal attack along the dark squares. Rooks are clumsy and ineffective without open files; even more so, and also vulnerable to attack, when they are surrounded by friendly forces.

I viewed the text move as necessary so as to protect against White's ♗f4 threat with ...e5, but it has the unpleasant drawback of allowing White's next move. I cannot remember why I rejected playing the principled 13...♖d8 first. Play might continue with 13...♖d8 14 ♕e2 ♘e8 15 ♗g5 when I would not mind playing 15...f6 and ...e5 depending on where White settled his bishop.

14 a5

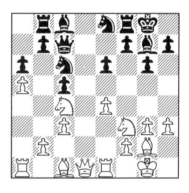

This effectively stops my intended ...b5 break. Clearly, White has the advantage. Suddenly my pieces are uncoordinated and White has obtained a good outpost on c4 for his knight. But let's closely examine the imbalances by doing a reconnaissance of the position. The knight on e8, although decentralized, fights for the control of d6. The rooks are not connected and they sadly lack scope. The one on f8 is particularly vulnerable to tactics. The bishop on c8 likewise lacks scope and the c5-pawn is defenceless. White possesses all the trumps including a simple but effective plan of developing the bishop to e3, redeploying the queen to a4 and repositioning the queen's rook to d1 to secure the control of the only open file. Practically speaking, Black is positionally lost. He really has no good options left except the text move:

14...e5 15 ♗e3

White gains a tempo with this move but I prepared a tactical solution to the threat against my c-pawn.

15...♗e6

Judging from his facial expression, this tactical resource seemed either underestimated or unexpected.

16 ♕e2

I thought White's best was 16 ♘fd2 ♖d8 17 ♕a4 ♘b8 with a big pull.

16...♗xc4

An interesting alternative is 16...♘d4, a move that would normally shock an unexpected opponent. If 17 cxd4 cxd4, Black regains his piece with equality. It would have been good for the psyche as it needed serious lifting at this point. The knight incursion into White's camp highlights the defect of

his choice of protecting the knight on c4 with ♕e2 instead of the more natural ♘fd2. It is a very active way of protecting c5 and sets White concrete problems.

This kind of move is unexpected because the mind cursorily dismisses any move that puts a piece under danger of capture by a pawn. If a move like this is found, usually it's by the player who has the opportunity to place the piece in danger. The other player who has the option to capture hardly considers these types of candidate moves because his mind simply dismisses them as impossibilities. *Finding these pseudo-impossibilities over the board will secure easy escapes from lost positions and reward the determined player with unexpected points.*

I did not consider 16...♘d4 simply because I was not actively looking for it. I was so drawn to the idea of eliminating White's a-pawn at the earliest possibility, since it had been severely cramping my queenside ambitions, that I ignored looking for much better options. 16...♗xc4 was motivated by a bias which received its justification from the moves played earlier. Again, the human tendency to bring over historical data into the move selection process only precipitated negative influences towards a poor choice in this instance.

17 ♕xc4 ♘xa5 18 ♕xc5 ♘c6 19 ♖ed1 ♘f6

Good thing I had this move. Now

the rook on f8 feels a little more comfortable.

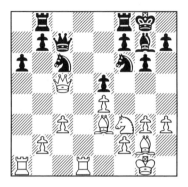

20 ♘e1 ♖fd8 21 ♕b6 ♕e7

The alternative try is 21...♖xd1, and here 22 ♕xc7 ♖xa1 23 ♔f1 ♘e8 gives Black a nice advantage. In this position, his king is safer than White's.

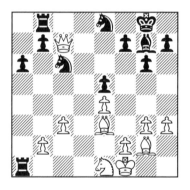

However, White can simply ignore the queen offer and proceed cautiously with 22 ♖xd1 ♕c8 23 ♘d3, retaining a slight advantage.

It is my observation that players below 2200 are somewhat afraid to give up their queen for two rooks. A feeling of discomfort usually dominates our demeanour when the queen leaves the board. Improvers should welcome the experience, whenever the opportunity arises, to play without the queen especially against strong opposition. I guarantee invaluable lessons will be the by-product of the experience which will serve you well in future contests.

A keen understanding of the imbalances which make exchanges favourable will give you additional firepower in your arsenal. Just being somewhat aware of an exchange possibility gives the watchful player an extra edge. In our experience, we give up our queens only when forced while under untenable conditions, with the idea of limiting damage to our game. Giving up the queen for two rooks or even for three minor pieces should always be part of our chess thinking process.

22 ♗c5

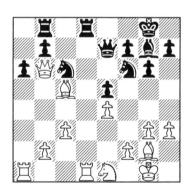

I saw the attack on my queen as an enticing continuation for White but did not fear it. In fact, I wanted him to do it because it would impede the retreat of the queen on b6 and I thought I could trap it after 22...♕e6. So the move 21...♕e7 was a subtle provocation, thinking that the resulting position would be good for me. Not taking the precaution of falsifying your ideas by finding the best moves for your opponent can be very hazardous.

22...♕e6

Once again, Black can first exchange rooks with 22...♖xd1 23 ♖xd1 ♘d7 24 ♗xe7 ♘xb6 and White must be alert to avoid the inaccurate 25 ♗d6?! (25 ♗g5 instead is marginally better for White), otherwise Black will stand slightly better starting with the annoying pin by 25...♖d8 26 ♖d3 ♘c4 27 ♗a3 ♘xa3 28 bxa3 ♔f8.

23 ♖xd8+ ♘xd8 24 ♕xe6 ♘xe6 25 ♗d6

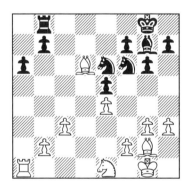

To be honest, I overlooked this move in my analysis of 21...♕e7. I simply did not go as far in my calculations. In most cases, it is not the inability to see far ahead, but rather the failure to look far ahead that causes us to miss moves giving our opponents the advantage. Luckily, in this instance, the move only looks good but it does not win on the spot for White. However, it disturbed me during

the game because I failed to see it as a plausible continuation for White when I played 21...♕e7. I had to settle myself before I could refocus my concentration. I had been moving rapidly in the last four moves as if driven by the momentum of haste. Prior to this position, I offered a draw hoping that my opponent, with this being the final round, would want to retire early. There was practically nothing for him to gain but only much to lose. My opponent, who is a titled player, was motivated to play on for a win because of his loss in the morning round, a fact he casually admitted to me after the game. But I am sure the rating disparity between us was a more plausible consideration in his refusal to retire the game early.

25...♖e8

One positive for using the MonRoi electronic scoresheet is that it records how much time is spent on any given move. The printed scoresheet indicates that it took me only 57 seconds to decide on this move, and the speed to which it was derived somewhat annoyed my opponent.

I believe he judged the position after 25 ♗d6 to be winning for him in his calculations. This faulty judgment likely motivated the sequence of exchanges he started on move 23. Otherwise, why would he allow the exchanges when he was unwilling to yield a draw? But it is to his credit that he got this far in his over-the-board analysis. I, on the other hand, indifferently stopped my calculation before 25 ♗d6. The shock reminded me during the game that his calculation horizon was farther than mine. I resolved to be extra careful from hereon.

Here you see that blunder-proofing your game and decisively exploiting blunders of your opponents fall short in the struggle to win games against stronger players. A necessary element to your improvement scheme is the ability to judge positions correctly. Being able to calculate deeper and wider many moves ahead is not enough. You do not get points for long calculations, only lost time and energy. But long calculations coupled with precise evaluations of positions will enable you to leapfrog most players. A crucial aspect of our game needing careful nurturing is the ability to see with clarity who stands better at the farthest point when calculating long variations from any given start position. Be forewarned, however, that depth is secondary only to sterling precision in chess evaluation.

26 ♗xe5 ♘xe4

Here my opponent took almost

three minutes deciding on his next move. I was not sure if he totally missed this resource. I believe I offered a draw again around this point.

27 ♗xe4

If 27 ♗xg7, then Black has 27...♘xg7 easily restoring material equality.

27...♗xe5 28 ♗xb7 ♖b8 29 ♘d3

White took five minutes and 29 seconds on this move. During the game, I thought this was his most active choice. But *Rybka* thinks 29 ♗xa6 ♖xb2 30 ♘d3 is much stronger and possibly gives White a winning advantage.

29...♖xb7

After this move, both chess engines think the position is now equal. Coincidentally, I also started feeling confident about my drawing prospects at this point. Drunk with the success of my narrow escape, my concentration began to drift away from the board. I was prematurely reflecting on my good fortunes and my potential FIDE rating. Later that evening at the hotel I discovered that a draw in this game would have given me a rating of 2244, just 56 points shy of the FIDE Master title.

30 ♘xe5 ♖xb2 31 ♖xa6 ♘g5

FM MacIntyre sheepishly told me during a brief post-mortem that he overlooked this move. He spent over 18 minutes for his response against the threat on h3. During his entire rumination, I witnessed an array of facial expressions betraying his mental state and his assessment of the position. At one point, he almost picked up the h-pawn only to notice just before making contact with the pawn that it was a blunder.

Make a note of this position because our thoughtless tendency is to actively protect the pawn by attacking the attacker. The brain has this in our memory bank as a stock response during time pressure. And at most other times it works well but not here because of the added pressure on f2 after ...♘h3+.

32 ♔g2

Despite his pawn advantage, you can see White is feeling some heat. I began to enjoy deciphering the now

familiar facial gymnastics punctuated by some eye rolling my opponent was putting on as he struggled for a viable defence.

32...♘e4

So how should White continue? I really thought I was better here. It is amazing how a positive thought could suddenly enthuse one to overestimate his chances. Taking into account my modest goal of halving the point, the turn of events made me feel I was about to win the struggle. *Premature elation like this one, if you are not careful, can blind you to lurking dangers.*

33 ♔f3 ♘xc3

33...f5!? was a possibility but I was afraid of the c-pawn reaching glory land. It turns out Black easily draws in this line according to *Fritz* and *Rybka*. The text move draws as well.

34 ♖a8+ ♔g7 35 ♖a7

Here I had a pleasant choice between 35...♔f6 and 35...♘d1. Both moves draw easily, with 35...♔f6 the surest route. In the game, I had planned to continue with 35...♘d1. In my impatience, I lost my sense of danger.

You can never let your guard down during any struggle, especially at critical junctures, until a conclusion is reached with either a resignation or a peaceful handshake. *Learn to identify these critical moments in the game because they deserve extra thinking time and sharper concentration.*

35...♖b5?

The first serious blunder in the game – totally inexcusable. I succumbed to a tactical hallucination. Why I did not continue straight away with 35...♞d1 is beyond me because I foresaw and settled for the line when I chose to continue with 33...♞xc3.

What happened here reveals a typical flaw in amateur chess thinking. I was about to play 35...♞d1 when I noticed a tactical trick where I thought I could win the knight on e5 if the rook took on f7. You can only imagine my horror when I realized the mistake, but this was not until the simple 38 ♖e6 appeared on the board. My mistake in

the execution of this phase of the game was failing to slow down my pace and failing to check carefully a new continuation. Beware of new opportunities suddenly appearing on the board without judiciously establishing the truth behind them.

A crucial axiom to note is *never change plans midway through a critical sequence without thorough checking.* I am sure you've had a similar experience before. Before you misunderstand my point, please allow me to further clarify it. I am not against looking for new opportunities while in a middle of a critical sequence. I am simply arguing that one must always defer to the first idea before changing its contours once its execution has commenced. The reason is simple. There was considerable time invested in the birthing of the first idea. And in practice we tend to recklessly exempt the new idea, when taken as a substitute course, from the application of the same rigor of investigation as with the original idea. We often point the blame to the practical constraint imposed by the clock.

35...♔f6 36 ♞xf7 ♞d1 37 ♞d6 ♖xf2+ 38 ♔e4 ♔e6 39 ♞c4 ♞c3+ 40 ♔e3 ♖f7 was the cleanest path to the draw. After the knight captures on f7, it is far removed from the defence of the f2-pawn. As soon as this pawn falls, the draw becomes unavoidable.

36 ♖xf7+ ♔g8 37 ♖e7 ♔f8 38 ♖e6

All hopes of obtaining a draw disappeared. I had simply missed this move, which adequately defends the knight. Had I invested more time falsifying my idea, the discovery of the refutation 38 ♖e6 would certainly have prompted me to abandon the erroneous plan of winning the knight. More importantly, the discovery would likewise have forced me to return to the original plan, which we now know to be sufficient for a draw.

38...♖d5?

I have said it before and it bears repeating. Blunders usually come in pairs and the resulting dire situation becomes impossible to recover from especially when they occur in succession. The sad part is that I saw the possibility for White to give up the knight for two pawns, only to dismiss it because I thought he didn't have the guts to do it.

The defensive 38...♔g7 was necessary, and Black can still probably draw.

39 ♘xg6+ hxg6 40 ♖xg6

The turn of events had become dispiriting. I could not focus on the current task. My mind was still thinking

about the missed opportunity with 35...♔f6 followed by 36...♘d1. The game is far from over, but in my mind it was. From here on, I was playing like I was already lost. My play was a reflection of how I felt about my position. The feeling was a direct result of my poor endgame knowledge. I was fooled into believing White's idea was indeed correct and winning. Both players from here simply acted out what they believed to be true with the position.

If I were a machine, I could easily forget the wasted chances moves earlier. *One way of forgetting bad memories is to pretend that the current board position is the game starting position.* No emotional baggage lingers to burden your psyche because there is no move history of lost opportunities. In chess, lost opportunities are better forgotten than remembered because of the pestering damage it cultivates in the mind. Only present and future opportunities matter so dwell more on them.

40...♖f5+

40...♘d1 would allow Black to fight on. If 41 ♔g2, then Black has 41...♔f7 42 ♖g4 ♖f5 43 ♖f4 ♖xf4 44 gxf4 ♔f6 and he can still probably hold with best play. The line 41 g4 ♖d2 42 h4 ♖xf2+ 43 ♔e4 ♖a2 also gives Black drawing chances.

The rest of the game underscores my lamentable endgame skills. Against this level of opposition, you cannot leave this part of the game ignored. It was fitting that this was the final game of the tournament as it became the last thing clearly etched in my memory. And so it has become the first thing I know I have to correct before the next contest. I am eager more than ever to incorporate endgame study into my regimen.

41 ♔g2 ♘d5 42 ♖g4 ♖e5 43 ♖d4 ♘e7 44 h4 ♖a5 45 g4 ♖a3 46 h5 ♔g7 47 f3 ♘g8 48 ♖d7+ ♔h6 49 ♖d6+ ♔h7 50 g5 ♖a7 51 ♔g3 ♘e7 52 ♔g4 ♘g8 53 f4 ♖b7 54 h6 ♖b5 55 ♔h5 ♖c5 56 ♖d7+ ♔h8 57 ♖f7 ♖b5 58 f5 ♖e5 59 f6 ♖e6 60 ♔g6 1-0

Because of this loss and the way it came to be, at that moment the entire tournament felt like a big disappointment for me. On the brighter side, the disappointment signalled my strong desire to do better next time and the feeling of being able to.

Chapter Four

Pan-American Continental Championship, November 2008

I originally did not plan to play in this event. Other plans were made to play in the North American FIDE Invitational in Skokie, Illinois, and my participation there was negotiated with the organizer shortly after the New England Masters concluded. November being my birth month feels just a little more special than other months. It is also the birth month of my mother who was living with us then. The problem with the Chicago event was the timing. My youngest sister Tess, a British citizen, surprised us by her intention to visit and for some very honourable reason decided to time her arrival for our mother's 81st birthday anniversary. Unfortunately for me the Skokie event begins on mom's birthday, which explains the hasty decision to cancel and to enter instead in the Pan-American scheduled early in the month. I was ready to miss the milestone but not my darling sister's visit.

The continental championship is a unique tournament for various reasons. Players who wish to play in it must be endorsed by their respective national federations. The winner of the event gets seeded into the World Cup and is awarded the grandmaster title by virtue of this one victory without regard to rating or earned norms. The 2008 edition was in sunny and gorgeous Boca Raton, Florida. What better excuse is there to feel the sun's warmth in the fall than a chess tournament of this significance? By all counts, however, I was not ready for this tournament and it showed.

My opponent in round five was IM Blas Lugo, who has earned one GM norm in the 90's. He grew up and learned chess in Cuba, but now runs the thriving Miami Chess Academy and is the force behind the popular annual Miami Open.

A.Hortillosa-B.Lugo
Boca Raton 2008
Semi-Slav Defence

1 ♘f3 d5 2 c4 c6 3 e3 ♘f6 4 ♘c3 e6 5 d4 ♘bd7 6 cxd5 exd5 7 ♗d3 ♗d6 8 0-0 0-0 9 a3 ♖e8 10 ♕c2 ♕e7 11 ♗f5 ♘f8 12 ♗xc8 ♖axc8 13 ♗d2 ♘g6 14 ♕f5 ♗b8 15 ♖ac1 ♖cd8 16 g3 ♘e4 17 ♖c2 ♖d6 18 ♕h3 ♘f8 19 ♕g2 ♘d7 20 ♘h4 ♕e6 21 ♘f3 f5 22 ♘e2 ♕f7 23 ♖fc1 g5 24 ♖f1 ♖g6 25 ♗c1 ♗d6 26 ♘e1 h5 27 f3 ♘ef6 28 ♘d3 h4 29 b3 hxg3 30 hxg3 ♕e7 31 a4 ♔g7 32 ♔f2 ♗a3 33 ♗d2 f4 34 ♘exf4 gxf4 35 ♘xf4

We join the action here. I had just given up a knight for two pawns to avoid immediate defeat. Clearly, Black enjoys a big lead and is winning. Meanwhile, the knight on f4 is attacking the rook on g6.

35...♖h6

Black is eager to finish off White in short order and he intends to double up rooks on the h-file. My next move

was practically forced but it came with a latent swindle waiting to materialize if Black continued in a natural manner.

36 ♖h1 ♖xh1?!

Better and safer was 36...♖eh8 when the resulting exchange leaves Black controlling the h-file.

37 ♕xh1

So far so good. I quickly recaptured on h1 so as to push my opponent to continue by momentum without giving him time to check for any lurking danger after his natural-looking follow-up.

37...♖h8??

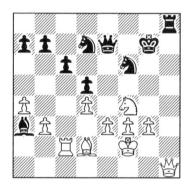

This was played quickly, even though Black was not under time pressure. This is the swindle or tactical opportunity that I saw when I played 36 ♖h1. There's no rational explanation for the blunder except that he got careless. In my mind, the seed of the error was planted in his previous move. Be careful with those natural-looking moves as they can be fraught with danger.

38 ♕xh8+ ♔xh8 39 ♘g6+ ♔g7

My opponent offered me a draw here and I thought about it for some time. Seeing that I had two passed pawns and a rook for two knights, I rejected the offer. It is not every day that you get to reject a draw offer from a strong IM.

40 ♘xe7 ♗xe7 41 g4 ♔g6 42 ♖c1

Preventing ...c5 with 42 b4 might be more accurate but I was in a hurry to activate my rook.

42...c5 43 ♖h1 cxd4 44 exd4 ♘b8

Black wants to reposition the knight to c6 to pressure d4 and to control more squares on the queenside.

45 ♖h6+ ♔g7 46 g5 ♘g8 47 ♖e6 ♘c6 48 f4

48 ♗e3 would be careless because 48...♔f7 traps the rook.

48...♘xd4

Black has made a practical decision of recouping one of the pawns but at the price of giving up two pieces for my rook. I evaluated the exchange to be advantageous to White. I also thought Black was simply trading one disadvantage for another but with a net gain of a slightly better drawing chance. He correctly chose a much better option, sensing that my endgame knowledge compared to his was vastly inferior.

This kind of over-the-board wisdom only comes after years of tournament experience. This is what I call game strategy to differentiate it from chess strategy. It does not involve positional considerations or exploitation of weak squares or badly placed pieces.

49 ♗c3 ♔f7 50 ♖xe7+ ♘xe7 51 ♗xd4 ♘c6 52 ♔e3 ♔g6

The position looks quiet, but had someone tapped my shoulder and said "White to play and win," the prompting alone would have led me to check one obvious forcing move. During the game this move did not even occur to me as possible. In this instance, and in similar cases, the brain somehow inexplicably ignores the move as if it is not even legal.

The tap on the shoulder would have led me to 53 ♗xa7!, winning right away. IM Lugo showed this move to me immediately after we agreed to a draw. I was too tired to feel annoyed. Surprisingly, it took *Rybka* more than a minute to find it. If Black takes with 53...♘xa7, the king invades decisively on d4 and the d5-pawn falls and with it the game. Play may continue as in 54 ♔d4 ♘c6+ 55 ♔xd5 ♔f5 56 ♔c5 ♘d8 57 a5 and White wins.

White's idea is to continue with b3-b4, b4-b5 and a5-a6 creating an unstoppable passed pawn.

One important lesson to learn from this endgame is this: *concrete variations are far more important in the endgame than hunches.* In the majority of cases, the winning plan is best arrived at by imagining preferable conditions for your pieces on the board. By that I mean where they should be and which ones ought to stay on or off the board, not just for you but for your opponent as well. For the above idea to work in this game, Black's king must be incapable of aiding the knight in stopping the queenside pawns. It is crucial that White's king must be on the same side where the opponent's remaining piece is defending. *If you can successfully split your opponent's defensive*

resources between two areas of concern, the winning task becomes much easier.
53 ♗c3 a6 54 a5 ♔f5 55 ♗d2 ♔e6 56 ♔d3 ♔f5 ½-½

We were both too tired to continue and agreed to a draw here. One last try to win is to aim for b4-b5 and invade via b4 at the right moment. A possible line is 57 b4 ♔g6 58 ♔c2 ♔f5 59 ♔b3 ♘e7 60 b5 ♔e6 61 ♔b4 ♔d6 62 ♗c1 ♘f5 63 ♗b2 ♘e7 64 ♗d4 ♘f5 65 g6 ♔e6 66 g7 ♔f7 67 bxa6 bxa6 68 ♔c5 ♘e7 69 ♔d6 ♘g6 70 f5 ♘f4 71 f6 and White wins.

Game 29
R.Barros-A.Hortillosa
Boca Raton 2008
Nimzo-Indian Defence

1 d4 ♘f6 2 c4 e6 3 ♘c3 ♗b4 4 ♕b3 c5 5 dxc5 ♘c6 6 ♗d2 ♘d4 7 ♕d1 ♗xc5 8 e3 ♘c6 9 ♘f3 0-0 10 ♖c1 ♖e8 11 ♗e2 b6 12 0-0 ♗b7 13 a3 a5 14 ♕c2 ♖c8 15 ♕b1 ♗d6 16 ♖fd1 ♘e5 17 ♘b5 ♗b8 18 ♘e1 ♘fg4

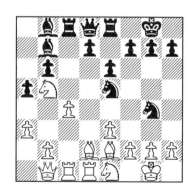

After 18...♘fg4, Black can claim an edge. White is in a predicament, and after the subsequent weakening of his kingside, I struck with a knight sacrifice.

19 g3 ♕f6 20 f4 ♘xh2 21 ♔xh2 ♕h6+ 22 ♔g1 ♕h1+ 23 ♔f2

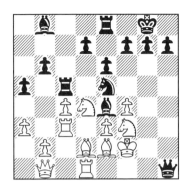

30...♘g4+??

Didn't I say blunders come in pairs? This is the move that gives away all the advantage and some more. Black can still fight on with 30...♕h3 31 ♗f1 (31 ♕xe4 allows a pretty finish with 31...♘g4+ 32 ♔g1 ♕g3+ 33 ♔h1 ♘f2 mate) 31...♘g4+ 32 ♔e2 ♗xf3+ 33 ♘xf3 ♕h1 as he gets to save his queen.

31 ♔g3

The sudden turn of events rattled me silly. I resigned in defeat after suffering for another 18 moves:

31...♕h5 32 ♕xe4 ♘f6 33 ♕b1 ♕g4+ 34 ♔f2 ♕h3 35 ♖g1 ♖h5 36 ♔e1 d5 37 ♗f1 ♕h1 38 ♖xh1 ♖xh1 39 c5 bxc5 40 ♖xc5 ♘e4 41 ♖c1 e5 42 fxe5 ♗xe5 43 ♗xa5 ♗f6 44 ♔e2 ♗xd4 45 ♘xd4 ♖h2+ 46 ♔e1 g6 47 ♕d3 ♖xb2 48 ♘c6 ♘f2 49 ♕d4 ♖a2 1-0

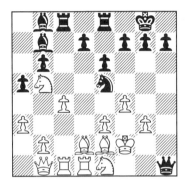

23...♕h2+

If I were playing a grandmaster, I would probably be happy to take a draw here; or maybe not.

Better is the immediate 23...♗e4 when play might continue as in 24 ♕a2 ♕h2+ 25 ♔f1 ♗f5 26 ♘g2 ♗h3 27 ♗f3 ♘xf3 28 ♔e2 ♕xg2+ 29 ♔d3, and Black is easily winning.

24 ♔f1 ♕xg3 25 ♖c3 ♕h3+ 26 ♔f2 ♕h2+ 27 ♔f1 ♖c5

Also possible is 27...♕h1+ 28 ♔f2 ♕h4+ 29 ♔f1 ♘g4 30 ♗xg4 ♕xg4 with a big edge for Black.

28 ♘d4 ♕h1+ 29 ♔f2 ♗e4?!

This is inaccurate but not quite a blunder. The more direct 29...♕h4+ 30 ♔f1 ♘g4 31 ♗xg4 ♕xg4 32 e4 ♖h5 is totally winning.

30 ♘ef3

Game 30
M.Lucente-A.Hortillosa
Boca Raton 2008

I had been chasing the white king

from g1 to c3 for some 10 moves before we got to this position. And more chasing followed:

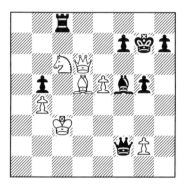

56...♕e3+ 57 ♔b2 ♕d2+ 58 ♔a3 ♕c1+ 59 ♔b3

How should Black continue? Bear in mind my king is also insecure. If White is allowed to check on f6, my king is a goner. Having done a good reconnaissance of the position earlier I was able to establish that White could not be accorded the check. This means the task of driving the white king to a corner should be carried out only with checks. One key data on the board that helped me figure out the moves is the

blockading function of the knight on c6. This knight effectively disbars the rook from entering the fray.

I cannot stress enough the importance of board reconnaissance as an important element of the chess thinking process. The by-product of this process step is the indispensable continuous data update you get from its execution. Another key observation gathered during the reconnaissance is the overprotection of the knight by the bishop and queen. It came to me early in the middle of the chase that if I could engineer the successful deflection of the bishop away from its defence, then I would win the knight as long as my queen was already attacking it before the deflection occurs.

Late in the chase as I was trying to figure out a mate involving my bishop, I saw another subtle characteristic of the position which escaped my notice earlier. Being aware of these ideas, I harassed his king and aimed for this very position shown above.

The queen and rook are now lined up against the knight. The only problem left to solve is how to deflect the bishop while not allowing the fatal check on f6. So, the return of the bishop to the e6-square actually came quite naturally:

59...♗e6!

However, it did not occur to me until I made the move that the bishop did not have to be deflected for the idea to work. It only needs to be pinned.

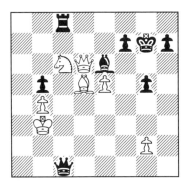

60 ♗xe6 ♖xc6 1-0

Seeing that he was losing the bishop too, my opponent resigned.

My last round game was against the illustrious USCF Executive Director, Bill Hall, who sports a ranking of Expert. He participated in the tournament primarily to obtain a FIDE rating, which in fact he succeeded in doing.

Game 31
A.Hortillosa-B.Hall
Boca Raton 2008

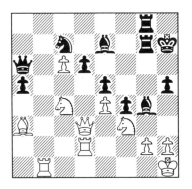

The game had developed into a King's Indian via a non-standard move order. I had been doing most of the pressuring in the last fifteen moves or so, and when a pseudo-opportunity arose, Black without any hesitation took it and played 36...♖dg8.

Sadly for him, it was not real counterplay but a mere precursor to a blunder. Since I had more time whereas he had literally a couple of minutes left before reaching time control on move 40, I spent it wisely labouring to understand what he was playing for and to see if I could lay a trap for him. This is an example of employing successfully the technique of idea falsification, not yours but your opponent's. If you are facing a threat, see if you can let the threat continue to its fruition as if you haven't seen it. Meanwhile, figure out if you can falsify his threat with a counter strike that actually works when ignored. There is something to be said about helping your opponent to blunder as a game strategy. Only be sure that the harm he is threatening to inflict on your position is indeed just a falsity.

To design a potent response, I first initiated the process of understanding the point of Black's last move, a sophisticated form of reconnaissance. My investigation revealed the following: Black intended to take the knight with ...♗xf3. He reasoned I could not take back with the queen because then the other knight on c4 would hang as it is under surveillance by the queen on a6. However, if I were to recapture instead with gxf3, then the opened file would endanger my king. Having understood his threat I looked to see if there was anything I could do to nullify his threat. Next, I reviewed my to-do list based on my reconnaissance of the position. I wanted to save the passed c-pawn if I could while defending the knight on c4.

Naturally, these deliberations led me to my next move. But first I had to certify by concrete calculation the chosen path of negation to Black's idea of capturing on f3. I suspected that Black would fall into my trap because he had little time to uncover the hidden danger.

37 ♖b6

The text move was my refutation of Black's idea. Black clearly saw my threat of ♖b6 menacing his queen off the f1-a6 diagonal with the idea of relieving the pressure on the pinned knight, but chose to ignore it so he could continue on with his plan. Whose threat is more fatal or which one will come through first? He wrongly concluded that allowing 37 ♖b6 would only strengthen his plan since it would leave my back rank weak and that I would really be forced to recapture with my queen. The respite would give his own queen the time to evade the rook's threat by capturing my knight on c4. This sequence of moves would yield him a full piece. Was his idea correct? Yes, but only to a certain point. He

was correct about the forced queen recapture but he overlooked one important data point on the board. Let's continue with the game to see what that point is.

37...♗xf3 38 ♕xf3

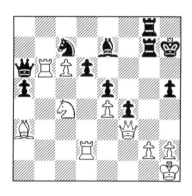

Black must have been thrilled to see that things were moving just as he wanted it to with the queen recapture. Now he could take the undefended knight on c4, but could he? Just before my opponent could pick up his queen, he noticed that with the bishop gone there appeared a nasty mate threat on h5. This was the negation I found once I understood the motivation behind his 36th move. His queen, therefore, had no time to either capture on c4 or save herself: if 38...♕xc4 then 39 ♕xh5 mate.

Seeing his error, he shook his head and continued:

38...♖g5 39 ♖xa6 ♘xa6 40 ♗xd6 ♗xd6 41 ♖xd6 ♖b8 42 ♘xa5 1-0

Noticing that the back rank mate on b1 is easily parried with ♖d1, Black resigned.

Chapter Five

Mid-America Open, March 2009

I gained 33 USCF but only a paltry two FIDE rating points from this five-round tournament. However, this tournament has taken some historical significance in my chess improvement aspirations in many ways. For one, it was in this event where Chicago-based GM Dmitry Gurevich agreed to take me on as his apprentice. He correctly diagnosed what I needed to do to improve to the next level. He also noted my tactical abilities after seeing my game against FM Karklins in the second round, which was an indirect affirmation of my chess thinking process. The accrued benefits gleaned from this tournament would be seen in my performance in Skokie, Illinois, the following week.

My cordial first-round opponent hailed from Ohio and sported a respectable 2223 FIDE rating.

Game 32
C.Bixel-A.Hortillosa
St. Louis 2009

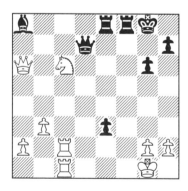

I had misplayed the opening phase and had to fight sharply in the middlegame for some improbable chances. This is an example of how positive attitude and fighting spirit can be harnessed to form a mighty partnership formidable enough to overcome even an opening disadvantage against an opponent much stronger than you. My opponent had begun to accumulate a time deficit starting in the middlegame tussle, and here he had less than a minute to get to the safe harbour of the first time control. In view of this, the following two checks were part of a good game strategy to get him closer to move 40 before his time expired.

37 ♕c4+ ♔g7 38 ♕c3+ ♖f6

After this block, he quickly pinned my rook not seeing my carefully concealed trap. It feels good catching your opponent succumbing to your good moves but it is even more satisfying when they plunge headlong into your traps.

39 ♖f1

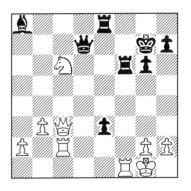

This kind of oversight is hard to see over the board especially when suffering under clock oppression. To help avoid it, simply do not allow yourself to get behind on time.

How do you finish White off? Do a terrain reconnaissance. Do you see any poorly defended pieces?

39...♕xc6

This shocker creates its greatest effect when made closer to end of time control. Finding the correct response with the extra pressure is near impossible. Also, shockers by their nature are very disconcerting. While it emboldens the dishing end, it seems to numb the receiving end into inaction. If you are on the unfortunate end and you have time on the clock, get up for some fresh air. Allow the brain to settle down from the shock before continuing. *If you dare continue your search for a response without stopping to regroup, what you will uncover are regrets not secrets.*

40 ♕d4

Does White escape defeat with this move? The queen maintains the pin and as a bonus the rook now attacks Black's queen. If White relied on the seemingly fortuitous arrangement of pieces as his way of escape, he was utterly negligent by failing to look deeper. He underestimated the significance of the queen capture which formed a murderous battery on the diagonal straight to his king. The decisive conclusion is this aesthetic in-between blocking move:

40...e2

Well, he reached time control with just about two seconds on the clock. With a new full hour, my opponent sat there for a long time thinking how he could extricate himself from this mess. For a while I thought I had missed a clever escape for him because he seemed to be looking at something deeply. I looked again, but I could not find any salvation for him as all lanes would end in a losing avenue. After about 20 minutes of thought, he nonchalantly played...

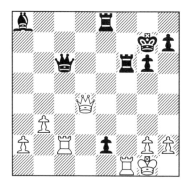

41 ♖xf6.

Saving him the embarrassment of a mate, I politely whispered mate on g2. And smiling, he quickly offered his hand in resignation. He sheepishly admitted that he was hoping for 41...e1♕+ when he would be winning. When this happens to you, do what he did. Had I been careless, I could have fallen easily to his mischief. Imagine how heartbreaking that would be? Chess can get cruel this way sometimes. But as a combatant, you owe it to yourself to keep fighting and giving your opponent problems to solve until the end. *As far as we know, no one wins by resigning.*

By the way, the tactical motif here is what I call piece blocking. My pawn on e2 blocks the rook's defence of g2 and

it threatens to capture on f1 with checkmate. In reality, my 40...e2 was a pure dual mate threat and only 41 ♕xf6+ could temporarily avert it.

Game 33
R.Murgescu-A.Hortillosa
St. Louis 2009

I had just played 42...♖b5-b7 and here I offered my 2267 USCF-rated opponent a draw. Of course, he declined the offer thinking he had the advantage because of my entombed bishop on f6. However, the bishop effectively holds off any h2-h4 pawn break. By the way, *Rybka* agrees with my assessment.
43 ♗d3

He accompanied his rejection with this polite remark, "You would not get offended if I keep playing, would you?" To which I responded with some confidence, "Of course, I wouldn't." And after some thought, he played the text move. This gave me the option of waking up my sleepy bishop with a pawn sacrifice. I was not sure if our short exchange gave him the idea to egg me into it or he simply overlooked the possibility.

43...♖c7+ 44 ♔b3 e4 45 ♗xe4 ♖c3+

Now, my rook also gets active.

46 ♔a4 ♖c4 47 ♗f3 ♖f4 48 ♖b3 ♖d4 49 ♔b5 ♔b7 50 ♔a5 ♖d2 51 ♖e3 ♖xh2 52 ♗e2 ♗e5 53 ♗a6+ ♔a7 54 ♗d3

Here I took the opportunity to seize the initiative with...

54...h5 55 gxh5 ♖xh5 56 b5 ♗c3+

This check is necessary to drive the king back to his third rank.

57 ♔a4 ♖h4+ 58 ♔b3 ♗e5

Now, I am the one in control of the game. And next move, it was his turn to offer me a draw. Well, you guessed it. I could not resist hearing our early exchange except this time the speakers of the lines were reversed. This was all done in jest.

59 ♖e4 ♖xe4 60 ♗xe4

After the exchange of rooks, it becomes a race back to the kingside.

60...g4 61 ♔a4 ♗d4 62 ♗g2 ♗b6 63 ♗e4 ♔b7 64 ♔b4 ♔c7 65 ♔c4 ♔d8 66

♗d3 ♔e8 67 ♗e2 g3 68 ♗f1 ♔f7 69 ♔d3 ♔f6 70 ♔e4 ♔g5 71 ♔f3 ♗f2 72 b6 ♗xb6 73 ♔xg3 ♔xf5 74 ♗h3+ ½-½

Even with a pawn deficit, White draws easily. But it is nicer to draw from a position of strength.

Game 34
A.Hortillosa-A.Karklins
St. Louis 2009
Latvian Gambit

---

1 e4 e5 2 ♘f3 f5

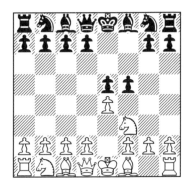

I did not expect to face the Latvian Gambit from the indomitable veteran FM Karklins. I found out later he specializes in many offbeat openings. So, what do you do when faced with such a challenge? Do not panic. Play solidly and develop sensibly and speedily.

3 ♘xe5 ♕f6 4 d4

I was just following known opening principles. There's nothing special about my moves in this game as I have no worked-out set up against the Latvian. It was not until later that GM

Gurevich gave me a coherent idea against this aggressive opening.

4...d5 5 ♘c4 fxe4 6 ♗e2

I was taking a modest approach. My goal was to complete kingside development by castling next move. The idea to open the f-file with f2-f3 was foreseen here.

6...♕d8 7 0-0 ♘f6 8 ♗g5 ♗e7 9 ♘bd2 0-0 10 ♗xf6 gxf6

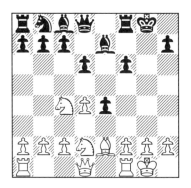

Black is not happy recapturing with the g-pawn but it is the lesser evil. He could not recapture with 10...♗xf6 because 11 ♘xe4 wins a pawn without compensation. Play may continue as in 11...d5 12 ♘xf6+ ♕xf6 13 ♘e3 with White being comfortably ahead.

11 f3 f5 12 fxe4 fxe4 13 ♖xf8+ ♗xf8 14 ♘xe4

I was aiming for this position when I gave up my bishop for his knight on f6.

14...♗g7

The idea to fork my knights with 14...d5 will not work because of the following line: 15 ♘e5 dxe4 16 ♗c4+ ♔g7 17 ♕h5 ♕xd4+ 18 ♔h1 when White is clearly winning.

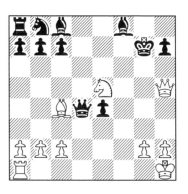

I really did not calculate concretely the ramifications of the sacrifice. I should have done some concrete analysis but I succumbed to laziness. Instead, I allowed some hazy algorithm as justification for allowing the possibility of Black forking my knights. Modesty aside, I saw the possibility of my rook controlling the f-file and with four pieces aggressively poised to attack the black king I felt confident I could mount a successful attack. I also correctly imagined Black's queenside forces a little slow in development to aid his king. I was banking on these assumptions to carry enough truth, which would bail me out when I took with 14 ♘xe4.

15 ♘g3 ♘c6 16 c3 d5 17 ♘d2 ♕g5 18 ♘f3 ♕e3+ 19 ♔h1 ♗e6 20 ♕c2 ♖f8 21 ♖f1

GM Gurevich in our multiple sessions from this particular game has suggested 21 ♖e1 as a better option, but at the board I didn't like the idea of allowing Black to sacrifice the exchange on f3 and ruin my pawn cover.

21...♛h6 22 ♗d3

This move is preparing to take on h7 next move. Already, I felt I was winning.

22...♗f6

When this move appeared on the board, I was certain he had seen my threat. The bishop now covers g5 and is effectively rendering my intended sequence toothless. It really is a multipurpose move as it prepares to redeploy to d6 after ...♗e7. Meanwhile, it allows Black to keep his bishop pair.

23 ♗xh7+

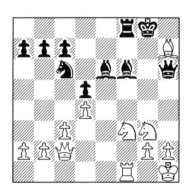

I looked at 23 ♘f5 for a long time before going ahead with my folly. Play

may continue as in 23...♛h5 24 g4 ♛h3 with White having a big advantage. But then I wondered if my original idea of taking on h7 would still work even with the bishop now on f6. When I saw I could win another pawn and the exchange for two pieces, I went for it. This error is an example of unrestrained exuberance unwarranted by the position. As amateurs we have a harder time tempering our reckless violent tendencies but to grow in chess, we must learn the art of trading smaller leads into bigger leads. Often, we embark on tactical skirmishes leading to nothing but the trading of a big edge for a smaller one.

This is also a case of foolishly getting too fancy. In fact, what I just did was complicate the win for White. I thought my two passed pawns would be enough to decide the day. I miscalculated the resisting powers of the two bishops and the pugnacious tenacity of Mr. Karklins. I was awed by this man's ability to stay concentrated for six long hours. I think he only stood up for a bathroom break once.

23...♛xh7 24 ♛xh7+ ♚xh7 25 ♘g5+ ♗xg5 26 ♖xf8 ♚g6

It was only after this move appeared that I began to realize the magnitude of difficulty I had brought upon myself. Black is threatening to trap my rook. It was here when the regrets started pouring in.

27 ♖f2 ♗h4

I still thought I could win the game

from this position. My simple plan is to unravel my position and push the pawns to promotion. This game has taught me more about endgames than all my other games combined. However, this is not the book for that kind of discussion. If you want to improve your endgame prowess, play either side and see if you can win or hold the game against a friend or chess engine. Sometimes it is your losses that teach you more about certain aspects of the game than your wins. This loss profits me more than the win earlier. Do not romanticize your wins because the only information these wins will give you are the errors of your opponents but not yours. You cannot gain from correcting their errors but you will by correcting yours.

28 ♖e2 ♗g4 29 ♖e3 ♗g5 30 ♖d3 ♘e7 31 h3 ♗d7 32 ♖f3 ♗b5 33 ♔h2 b6 34 ♘h1 ♘f5 35 g3 ♗e7 36 h4 c5 37 dxc5 bxc5 38 ♔h3 d4 39 ♘f2 ♘e3 40 g4 ♗f1+ 41 ♔h2 ♗xh4

Just thirteen moves from the last diagram, I blundered one of my pawns and lost shortly. I kept fighting for a draw but to no avail.

Chapter Six

North American FIDE Invitational March 2009

As mentioned earlier, I had originally planned to play in this 9-round IM norm invitational in November 2008. Just about four months after the Pan-American debacle, I finally showed up to this monthly series armed with a tuned chess thinking process. I've chosen three games that have instructional value for our purposes. I consider this event the toughest test of my chess thinking process so far.

After five rounds of play, only FM Felecan and I had a mathematical chance to earn a norm towards the International Master title. My loss to Felecan in the sixth round eliminated any sliver of contending for a norm. In the end, none of the norm hunters achieved the required score. FM Felecan narrowly missed his second norm by half a point. But he subsequently earned the required norms in the same series and is awarded the IM title this October.

My final score of 4 points garnered 59 USCF rating points, which brought my total gain in one month to 92. I also gained 26 FIDE points.

Let's start this chapter with my first ever win against an International Master in a rated event, FIDE or USCF.

Game 35
A.Hortillosa-M.Pasalic
Skokie 2009
Sicilian Defence

1 e4 c5 2 ♘c3

I sat down at the board intent on playing the Grand Prix Attack (GPA) in the event my opponent answered with 2...d6. White players disinclined to face the Sicilian Najdorf threaten to play the GPA and only revert to an Open Sicilian after flummoxed Black players choose a different Sicilian other than their favourite set-up. It is becoming a potent transpositional device employed by top players to get what they want in the opening. I had no such pretensions in this encounter.

2...e6

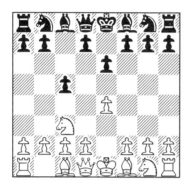

3 g3

Black's second move precludes the GPA version I like so I switched to the Closed Sicilian. It is known that the GPA with ♗c4 is ineffective against a set-up involving an early ...e6 because the central thrust ...d7-d5 can be accomplished in one move as Black has not wasted a tempo on ...d6 like in a Najdorf. I could still opt for an Open Sicilian with 3 ♘f3 and 4 d4 as such befits my style, but as yet I feel inadequately prepared to even try. In truth my unwillingness is a psychological issue more than reality. I am convinced by the inevitability of venturing out into the Open Sicilian realm if I hope to make progress beyond the 2200 level.

In anticipation I am slowly acquiring theory, and by next year it shall see its debut in my repertoire. I sometimes

dabble with the provocative 2...♘c6 3 g4 à la GM Suttles, but I have since limited the experimentation in games played with the Team 45 45 League at the Internet Chess Club.

3...♘c6 4 ♗g2 ♘f6 5 ♘ge2 a6 6 a4 d6 7 d3 ♕c7 8 0-0 ♗e7 9 h3 ♗d7

In this position, I wanted to play 10 g4 followed by ♘g3 and f2-f4 but Black's intentional delay in finding a home for his king prevented me from commencing this thematic idea. The g4 advance can become too loosening and the pawn itself can be a target for Black to latch on to after he castles queenside. I thought of developing the dark-squared bishop as a waiting move but I was not sure where it should go.

10 d4

My strong bias against moving the same piece twice in the opening before completing development kept me from reaching the decision to open the position without struggle. But seeing no obvious harm to my position with the advance to d4, I ignored the bias and bravely established contact with Black's forces. Looking back now I wish I had kept the position within the confines of a Closed Sicilian with 10 ♗e3. As you will notice in my subsequent moves, I could not commit to a plan and became very indecisive.

10...cxd4 11 ♘xd4 0-0 12 ♗e3

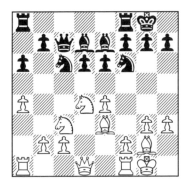

I hesitated with this move but the desire to complete queenside development prodded me. Now that Black has castled I felt that I should bring the knight back to e2 and continue with the familiar g3-g4 and ♘g3 idea. I did not have the courage to make it because it would look so frivolous and extravagant so I chose the obvious developing move.

12...♘e5

IM Pasalic hastened to show my erring ways with the quick knight hop to e5. Driving the knight away with f2-f4 forces it to a better square on c4. It will then force White to retreat the bishop back to c1 and render the g1-a7 diagonal vulnerable to Black's pieces, not to mention the dangerous pin against the knight on d4.

13 ♔h2

Preparing to play f2-f4 without worrying about the knight getting pinned by ...♛b6 in one possible line. It would be nice if White could play ♗g1 after ...♘c4, but the b2-pawn would object sternly.

13...♘c4 14 ♗c1 ♖ac8

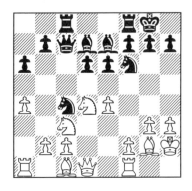

Notice that Black has gained time as my pieces are back to where they were before move 12, except the king. I evaluated this position to be a lot better for Black. Already, I was beginning to feel some pressure. However, I was determined not to get disheartened with my gloomy prospects so as not to drown my mind with negative vibes. I began searching for any redeeming possibilities in my position to stay within the grounds of positive territory.

15 b3

I considered 15 ♘ce2 first with the idea of continuing with 16 b3 ♘e5 17 f4 ♘c6 18 c4 when I thought White would be better. My evaluation is later proven slightly off target by chess engines. *Rybka* judges the position to be clearly equal. I like to have more space but when I get it I seem to overestimate my position. I do not mind surrendering to this bias at all because I tend to play better in positions which I have a happy disposition towards.

Only with a good reconnaissance would Black be able to find the best continuation here. With the knight being threatened, *what should Black play?* The knight has seven legal squares but only e5 seems attractive. Returning the knight to e5 would yield the initiative back to White after f2-f4. In addition he gets to place his bishop on b2 without difficulty achieving a good position with promising middlegame prospects. A proper reconnaissance would yield the undefended knight on c3.

15...♘e3

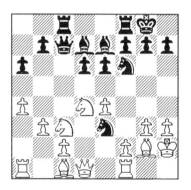

Nice. It's a move any master would easily find. Still, this type of move fascinates me because it does not come without effort. Who places a piece on a square attacked by a pawn? If you only do a cursory scan of the position, your mind will ignore such moves since it

has been conditioned to avoid danger. *Danger avoidance over time spawns biases.* But not all biases are harmful. A strong bias against moving pawns in front of a castled king is generally good and we have learned from numerous defeats to avoid them. However, some biases if not carefully considered will preclude us from finding those unusual moves that the position demands.

The instance of finding this move becomes possible only when the mind examines all legal moves, and it takes effort. One might argue that Black's move came out of necessity as he had to reject the unpleasant return of the knight to e5. Regardless, my failure to even consider it as a possible continuation for Black irritated me during the game. It's not just the move that bothered me, but more so the instance of failing to consider it. I am sure you see the difference.

16 ♗xe3 ♕xc3 17 ♖a2

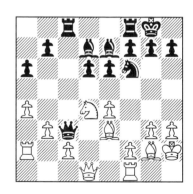

I like this move but *Rybka* prefers the more principled 17 ♖c1. The rook removes b2 from the black queen and looks with optimism to the possibility of doubling later to form a battery with friendly forces. My pleasant attitude over the future prospects of my position facilitated the finding of moves like ♖a2, a positive and forward-looking move.

17...♖fd8 18 ♘e2

The knight came back to e2 after all. After this, I felt better about my position.

18...♕a5 19 c4

The rook is finally liberated from its prison, eager to spring into action.

19...♗c6 20 ♕b1

I spent considerable time on my last six moves safely navigating the minefield caused by my lazy attitude in the opening, and now I only had three minutes and 54 seconds on my clock against 19 minutes for my opponent.

20...d5 21 cxd5 exd5 22 e5

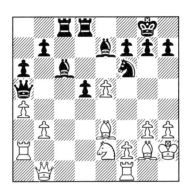

Now the d4-square is firmly under White's control.

22...♘e4 23 ♖c2

My decision to develop this rook on

the second rank earlier is proving brilliant.

23...♕c7

Who would think that the queen on a5 would run out of squares? Feeling unsafe alone, she quickly heads home to find safety among friends.

24 ♗d4

The threat to my e5-pawn was a welcome invitation to deploy my bishop on this fine diagonal. Already, I was seeing a bright future for the bishop.

24...♘g5

The agile knight quickly relocates to threaten the bishop from e6.

25 ♕c1 ♘e6 26 f4

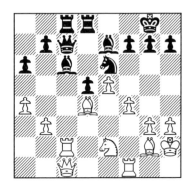

This is a necessary move to defend the e5-pawn because the bishop, its only defender, is threatened. It also adds to the agenda the annoying advance f4-f5 with tempo, which elicited a reaction weakening the dark squares around Black's king. Now the bishop's potential value relative to other pieces has increased, and to devastating effect later on.

26...g6 27 ♕d2

I decided to safely shore up the d4-square before I could retreat the bishop to b2. A premature ♗b2 will give Black the option to play ...d4 shutting off the bishop's access to the long diagonal. *Rybka* prefers 27 ♕e3 as it also threatens 28 ♗b6 winning the exchange. However, I did not want to give Black a reason to take on d4 because I valued my bishop to be better than his knight on e6. I was already thinking about an attack along the diagonal.

27...♗f8 28 h4

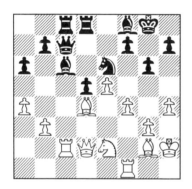

I wanted to get the edgy bishop into action and discourage the knight from taking the valuable bishop on d4. *Rybka* prefers the aggressive thrust 28 f5. It was hard to nudge the brain to get on the offensive at this point because I felt my pieces were not optimally placed for an immediate clash.

28...♖e8 29 ♗h3 ♕e7 30 ♗b2 ♖cd8

Black struggles, shuffling his pieces in a cramped position and getting ready to repel White's attack.

31 ♘d4 ♗d7

It was time to get the fireworks going with my next move:

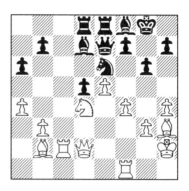

32 f5 ♘xd4 33 ♕xd4

The material count is equal but it is easy to see that White has a winning advantage. I could hardly suppress my excitement here but there was still some work to be done.

33...♕b4

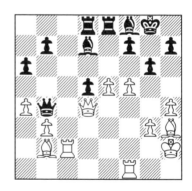

I saw this defensive idea while my opponent was thinking so I started looking for the most forcing continuation on his time. My opponent had used up his time advantage on the previous two moves and by the time he finally made this move, the time advantage had shifted to my side.

As every move changes the battle terrain, an update of the reconnaissance data is prudent. You do not want to miss important subtleties of the position. Also, ideas previously rejected as implausible might prove doable now due to favourable changes on the board. *What should White play here?*

34 ♖c4

It did not take me long to make this move on the board. I had debated between the somewhat "safer" continuation in 34 fxg6 and the text move as a response in case Black played the expected 33...♕b4. I had a hard time following on with the complications with the former option. In the end I chose the text move because of its clarity. Later analysis from *Rybka* confirms 34 fxg6 to be much stronger than what I played.

34...dxc4 35 e6

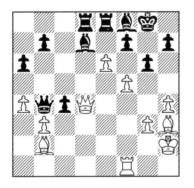

Here, as my opponent was thinking, I saw and feared 35...c3 so I began looking intensely at 36 exf7+. I began to entertain destructive thoughts bordering on cruelly judging my chess ability to that of a hopeless patzer. But before it could do any further damage, I got myself to focus on the task at hand encouraged by the slow reaction from my opponent, which I took to mean trouble for him. I mentioned this "possible" resource during the post-mortem, but did not get any positive indication that he even considered the move. By this time, he was dangerously behind on the clock. With less than 10 seconds left and just before I could figure out if 36 exf7+ would work for me, the losing continuation appeared on the board.

35...f6

Rybka confirmed 35...c3 to be the pragmatic choice. It would force White to find the only moves to finish on top. Play may then continue 36 exf7+ ♔xf7 37 fxg6+ ♔g8 38 ♕d5+ ♔h8 39 ♖xf8+ ♖xf8 40 ♕e5+ ♔g8 41 ♗xc3 ♕xc3 42 gxh7+ ♔xh7 43 ♕xc3 and White retains his advantage but winning will not be easy. For sure the emotional letdown would have disturbed my confidence level. Remain belligerently uncooperative and always strive to present your opponent with the most difficulty even if the chosen resistance loses in the end. *Give the annoyance factor the opportunity to disturb your opponent's rhythm of play.*

36 ♕xf6

Black is utterly defenceless so he goes for some tricks.

36...♕d2+ 37 ♗g2 ♕xg2+

Just like earlier, Black failed to

choose the most pragmatic choice in 37...♕xb2 to prolong the fight, since we were both in time pressure with each having under a minute left. The time control allowed us to increment our clock by 30 seconds every move.

38 ♔xg2 c3 39 ♕f7+ 1-0

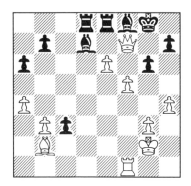

He resigned as mate was inevitable.

It is just most recently that I started firming up my repertoire as Black. Before 2009, I really didn't have a coherent repertoire. As Black against d4, I played the Queen's Gambit Declined, the Nimzo-Indian, the Bogo-Indian and the Queen's Indian. Somehow, I have never tried the King's Indian, the Benko, the Grünfeld or the Modern Benoni in tournament play – not even once to this day.

Part of this repertoire retooling process is the happy addition of the Semi-Slav after reading IM Vigorito's excellent book, *Play the Semi-Slav*. His discussion on move-order issues alone profoundly enabled my growing chess understanding because it opened my eyes to this aspect of opening play, a potent weapon at the beck and call of the masters. Nuances of move orders – how they influence one's opening choice and its execution is sadly beyond the interest horizon of amateur players.

Beginning this year, I resolved to widen just a bit my repertoire so I started absorbing the basic ideas behind these neglected openings. My goal was to slowly accrue specific knowledge of these openings including their typical plans, move orders and transposition lines over a period of one year.

Because of these purposeful efforts to remedy my incoherent repertoire, I have achieved some relative competence with regards to my openings though not quite reaching a respectable level as yet. As a secondary benefit, I no longer deal with indecision or apprehension over which defence to use against any of White's most popular openings.

Game 36
C.Boor-A.Hortillosa
Skokie 2009
Semi-Slav Defence

1 ♘f3 ♘f6 2 c4 e6 3 ♘c3 d5 4 d4 c6

By way of transposition, we reached a Semi-Slav structure with White having the first choice at determining the face of the subsequent struggle.

5 e3 ♘bd7 6 ♕c2

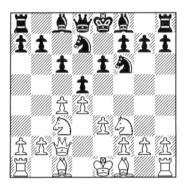

This move introduces the anti-Meran system and signals White's intention to possibly play the popular Shabalov-Shirov Attack: 6...♗d6 7 g4. Knowing that my book knowledge against this was inadequate, I chose what I thought to be a normal line. I was very wrong, of course.

6...dxc4?!

It is easy to confuse and mix up systems in the early stage of learning a new opening. Do not get too concerned when you find yourself in this predicament. The upside to this is that you will unlikely stumble blindly into the position again.

This is really how we should be "learning" openings as opposed to just "knowing" them. We acquire knowledge better and faster through "learning by doing" and not through "learning by knowing". This is better explained by the logical difference between these two statements: "I know golf because I watch golf on TV most weekends," and "I know golf because I play golf at the club on weekends."

There is a massive gap of usable knowledge between the two notions.

Besides offering the option of playing the aggressive g2-g4, the 6 ♕c2 line is also meant to prevent the very move I just made. My opponent told me rather nicely after the game that after I made the move, he was convinced I knew nothing of this particular opening scheme. We can only speculate if this conclusion dulled his sense of danger as his next moves seem to suggest.

7 ♗xc4 b5 8 ♗d3 ♗b7

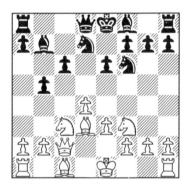

9 e4

Another good alternative available to White, owing to the placement of the queen on c2, is 9 ♘e4 ♘xe4 10 ♗xe4 ♖c8 11 ♗d2 intending to follow up with 12 b4 after which White gets a bind on the c5-square. This is a position aspiring Semi-Slav players need to know and must avoid. The positional pluses White gains are obvious.

9...a6

Preparing to enforce the standard break with ...c6-c5, but White was already getting on with his own agenda.

10 e5 ♘d5 11 ♘xd5 cxd5

This recapture entombs my bishop on b7, but the alternative in ...exd5 cannot be considered due to even more calamitous consequences. Already, I was feeling insecure about my position. With less that 15 moves played, I was forced to choose between equally harmful evils with which there was no hope of surviving unless a gift landed on my lap...

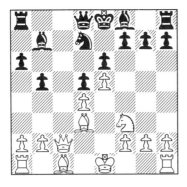

12 ♗xh7??

This move was played almost instantly, as if White had this capture in mind when he played e4-e5. As the shock of disbelief settled down, I began to question the accuracy of the move. The capture just didn't look right to the eyes. However, my hasty conclusion was not based on concrete lines but more on intuition. While not sure if Black was winning now, the earlier feeling of desolation slowly dissipated and was replaced with a feeling of relief slightly suppressed by a healthy tinge of suspicion. It is amazing how a positive outlook can suddenly make you see latent possibilities in your position.

Now that my opponent had time to reflect on his previous move, I waited for "tells" on his face to see if he also came to the same conclusion. I find this over-the-board technique useful and have been using it whenever there is opportunity. What I do is give my opponent time to falsify his own ideas in critical moments as he waits for my response. Sometimes the feedback is obvious and pronounced at the first moment the opponent notices the blunder. The body language signals can come in the form of a slow motion head-shaking or an audible grunt, or both. Even the calmer operators who are experts in suppressing their emotions are betrayed by the redness around their necks and on their ears. The window is very narrow so you have to pay careful attention and disguise your stares accordingly. Obviously, this technique cannot be used when you are both under time pressure, as you have no time to watch him and he doesn't have time to even realize his dire situation.

From my limited experience, the technique works very well when you are not in a state of panic induced by the clock. You have got to have the time to waste on gathering facial tells. Be warned as this can work both ways. Your opponent can also fake his misery either by a carefully choreographed head-shaking or some measured audible sighs all designed to encourage you to jump headlong into a pseudo-combination only to be caught in a cruel trap at the end.

Looking at the current position, notice that White's light-squared bishop on h7 is facing forcible eviction off the board. In addition, White's queen cannot detach contact with the stranded bishop, which effectively limits her scope to two squares, b1 and d3. Again, a good reconnaissance led me to:

12...♖c8

I have to assume that my opponent overlooked this in-between move in the short time that he took for his eleventh and twelfth moves. It was not difficult to see. He simply did not take the time to look. Elsewhere I said that blunders usually come in pairs or in succession. *If you realize you have just made one, get up, initiate a memory dump to clear your memory stores and return to the table as if you are starting the game afresh from the current position.* It is not easy so work hard on it.

13 ♕b1

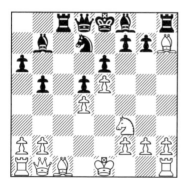

FM Boor made this move just as quickly as his previous one, except this time it was followed by a hint of disgust and disbelief over the conduct of his own play, I supposed. I got the "tell" I needed and wasted not a second more to investigate concretely the source of his disgust. The search for the refutation came to me quickly.

Be on the lookout for tactical opportunities when one or two known conditions for its presence exist on the board. Noticing the cornered queen and the double function it performs in defending both bishops, I concluded that enabling conditions in fact do exist for a tactical combination. *The formula starts with seeing that conditions exist, which then serves as a prompt for the brain to look for the puzzle solution.* At this point, the search for a tactical combination becomes a "Black to play and win" puzzle exercise.

The conditions serve also as the arbiter as to which side possesses the tactical opportunity. The conditions in this game are: inadequately supported bishop on h7 and overworked queen which also suffers from lack of habitable squares. *When you see a condition in your position, immediately make repairs before the hammer strikes hard.* Conditions also serve as reliable markers as to where the focal square of the combination resides. In this instance, the conditions only exist on the White side of the position so it is clear that Black is the one who has the tactical opportunity. Furthermore, the conditions point to c1 as the primary focal square and h7 as the secondary one. Taking on h7 first will doom the combination to failure because h7 is not the primary focal square.

Failure to notice these conditions often result in missed tactical opportunities leaving you guilty of negligence and feeling really dumb. Dealing with wasted opportunities is the hardest to pacify mentally and emotionally, especially when you have amassed advantages making you feel the rightful possessor of the win and the hallowed point. Some of these conditions surface or become evident only after a move or series of moves. *It is important to remember the dictum that every move alters the position; therefore, a proper reconnaissance must be taken at every turn if time permits.*

13...♖xc1+ 14 ♕xc1 ♖xh7

I offered my opponent a draw here, thinking incorrectly that the reversal of fortunes had merely allowed me to catch up with the material count. As far as having a winning advantage, it was a judgment I could not make for certain. The underestimation of my largesse was largely influenced by the entombed bishop on b7.

Correct evaluation of positions when material count is fairly equal remains a continuing struggle for me and for many others who are below master level. Often, this neglected chess skill leaves us lost without a functioning directional guidance when navigating turns and corners in the unmarked terrain of the chessboard. The consolation for me is that my chess style seems to limit the frequency of my wanderings into unclear lines. In the majority of cases, I am either clearly winning or simply busted.

However, if we want to make forward progress, we need to alleviate this sorry condition. I have begun to fix this aspect of my play with GM Dmitry Gurevich as my guide. We started working together after the Mid-America Open in St. Louis, Missouri, in March 2009. My relative success in this follow-up tournament is proof of my steady progress in this regard. He tells me this road is long and arduous based on what he sees in my game, but the finish line, though still afar, appears on the horizon. Believe me; I am inclined to agree with him. For you, however, the first concern is the successful scaling of the 2000 rating hurdle. To get you over it, you must correct foremost your blunder tendencies, which is the main objective of this book.

Returning to the game, a more precise continuation is 14...♗b4+ first before capturing the bishop on h7. You have to be sensitive to this kind of subtlety. When I realized how imprecise my move order was, I promptly gave myself a quick reminder to be careful from this point on and not be buoyed into carelessness by these ill-gotten gains. I said to myself, "You now have to work hard if you want to win this 'won' game."

15 ♕c2

My doubts about my position grew when my opponent rejected the draw offer with a move threatening my rook, suggesting his disinterest in a truce and his desire to fight to the end. My fear subsided when I noticed the move to be a positional error. As if in a stupor, my opponent continued his erring ways and essentially cancelled my previous imprecise move. White should play a2-a3 first to prevent the check on b4 before attacking the rook on h7. White could also just castle short, which would be far better than what he played.

15...♗b4+

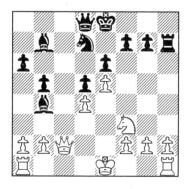

Not giving him another chance to tuck the king away to escape harassment.

I can only imagine the emotional burden my opponent was going through at this point. I am sure he intended to castle short after Black shuffled the rook to safety. What made him miss the developing check? For us, we need to be ever reminded that material threats are harmless if they can be nullified by intervening checks.

One of the fundamental first principles of chess I consider crucial to our development is that players take turns and can only make one move at a time. The turn to move is ceded only in a practical sense if the other player responds on his turn with a check. By the way, not all checks are equal. The check that cannot be parried by interposing another piece between the checking piece and the king is supremely valuable. A fork and double check are the ultimate forms of this type of check.

White missing the in-between check is a type of positional mistake I classify as "error in sequence". Masters know this and they invariably execute the right sequence almost in automatic fashion, but only when the psyche is undisturbed.

This malady is very familiar to us because we suffer the marks of it as well; in fact, more often. We are more prone to errors of sequence during episodes of emotional setbacks. *The most perilous time is immediately after the* instance of an emotional setback like squandering a winning advantage. The cure then is obvious – do a time out. We tend to self-destruct when the tables are turned against us. Just imagine the harm to the psyche when not more than three moves ago, White had already achieved a winning position. This is the same player who successfully rebuffed IM Young's ferocious attack the round before this, combining both active defence and a carefully crafted counter-attack to subdue the seven-time Illinois state champion in his area of strength.

16 ♔e2

The decision to bring the king forward is double-edged. While it develops the king's rook, the king itself is less safe on e2 than on f1.

16...♖h6

I like this move as it gives Black the extra option of playing ...f6 to undermine White's spearhead on e5.

17 a4?

This to me was the critical blunder. The move is not hard to understand as it facilitates the opening of the file for the rook; that is, if Black cooperates. White gambled recklessly here and in the process helped Black to activate his unopposed bishops raring to go on a king hunt. It's ironic that the blunder does not lose material but the consequences – placing the king's health in terrible jeopardy – are much more fatal. In the end, it is the unearthed light-squared bishop goaded with the lust to inflict harm which forced the monarch to enter a mating net near the middle of the board. It was at this point I began to really believe I was winning.

Rybka suggests 17 ♖hc1 ♗a5 18 ♕b3 as a viable effort to stay in the game, leaving Black with a slight advantage.

17...bxa4 18 ♖hc1 a5

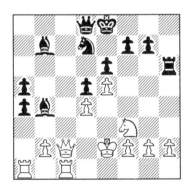

19 ♕xa4

The queen sortie looks attractive because it pins the knight but she has also left the defence of the king to the overworked steed. I am convinced White really thought his king stood safe behind an impregnable bulwark from attack. Otherwise, the prudent move is to ferry the king to safety with 19 ♔f1. And after 19...♗a6+, White has 20 ♔g1 limiting Black to a comfortable edge.

19...♗a6+

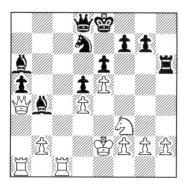

20 ♔e3

With the king running out of flight squares, his life just got much shorter. While this move is not forced because ♔d1 is also an option, it does force Black to proceed bravely and decisively if he wants to claim the prize.

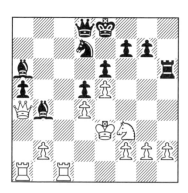

In positions like this one, pieces accrue varying qualitative values. Here, it is easy to judge that the rook on h7 is less valuable than the white knight on

f3 since the latter precludes the queen from invading on g5.

20...♖h4

Still, it took me a long time to make the temporary sacrifice because I had to circumspectly fact-check the follow-up. My time dangerously got low to less than 3 minutes when I finally made the move. If I could not get through to his king, my opponent's 50-minute advantage would probably win him the game. I wish I had the discipline and resolve of FM Albert Chow, a highly respected Chicago player. He told me he would rather lose on time than be rushed to make an embarrassing move.

21 ♘xh4 ♕xh4 22 ♕c2

His other try is 22 ♖c3 ♕e4+ 23 ♔d2 ♕xd4+ 24 ♔c1 ♗xc3 25 bxc3 ♕xc3+ 26 ♔d1 when Black ends clearly on top as well.

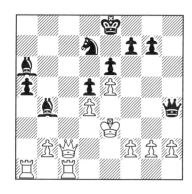

22...♘xe5

I took a huge deficit on the clock earlier while figuring out the surest path to a win after White accepted the rook offer on h4. Now, I am facing the paralyzing effect of severe time pressure. With practically no time left on the clock, I dished out this move secured by the knowledge that I was already winning. The clock forced me to quit looking for flashy mates.

A stunning move which I did not even consider during the game is 22...♗d2+.

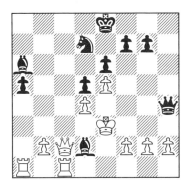

It doesn't matter how White responds to the check as all lines lead to checkmate: 23 ♕xd2 ♕e4 mate; 23 ♔xd2 ♕xf2+ 24 ♔c3 ♕e3+ 25 ♕d3 ♕xd3 mate; or 23 ♔xd2 ♕xf2+ 24 ♔d1 ♕f1+ 25 ♔d2 ♕e2+ 26 ♔c3 ♕e3+27 ♕d3 ♕xd3 mate. What stands out in this position is the role the pawn on a5 plays in all the mating variations. It is the silent hero of this game. In the variation actually played, it splendidly fulfilled its dutiful role of defending the bishop on b4 while shielding the other on a6. But in the 22...♗d2+ line, the humble pawn is even more indispensable in covering the escape square b4.

23 g3 ♕h6+

After 23 g3 the same idea with 23...♗d2+ 24 ♕xd2 ♕e4 also ends in

mate. If White takes the bishop with the king instead, then you get this mate: 23...♗d2+ 24 ♔xd2 ♕xd4+ 25 ♔e1 ♘f3.

24 f4 ♘c4+ 25 ♔f3 ♕h5+ 26 ♔f2 ♕xh2+
0-1

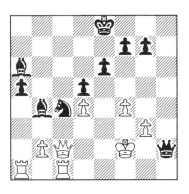

White resigned. Clearly, my opponent was off-form in this contest because it is nearly impossible to subdue a strong player of his calibre from an inferior position in under 30 moves. In his other games, he played but masterful chess. In the second round, he had the misfortune of losing on forfeit because he forgot to place his phone on mute. His draw in the first round and his loss to me in the fifth round mathematically killed his norm chances. If you get a chance to listen in to any of his post-mortems, do not let the opportunity go by. You would be glad you did.

The following game was played in the last round of the event. Since my opponent and I both stood at 3½ points apiece, the only thing left to fight for was reaching an even score of 4½ points out of nine. Being the higher-rated player, my opponent was in no mood for a draw. I had nothing to lose in playing for a win, but a draw would suit me just fine.

My research prior to the game found 17 games of his as White in my database. He opens with either 1 e4 or 1 d4 making any focused preparation harder for his opponents. For our game, I prepared mainly against 1 d4 and was expecting a 4 ♕c2 Nimzo-Indian, a line he had played in Round 1 of the tournament. His choice of the Closed Sicilian surprised me because he has shown a strong preference for the Open Sicilian in the majority of his games.

1 e4 c5 2 ♘c3 ♘c6 3 g3 g6 4 ♗g2 ♗g7 5 d3 d6

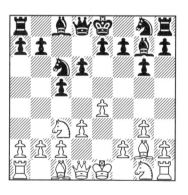

So far, we are in normal territory. White has a number of options with regards to the face and character of the ensuing struggle.

6 f4

White chooses the old main line. The popular 6 ♗e3 is the new main line to which Black has four equally playable responses: 6...e6, 6...♘f6, 6...e5 and 6...♖b8. I have tried all of them in my games, but usually prefer the flexible 6...e6.

My opponent's decision to eschew what current theory considers the most favourable line led me to suspect that he had something prepared, exploiting my unfamiliarity with the older line. So, I began to wonder what it would be.

6...e6 7 ♘f3 ♘ge7 8 0-0 0-0 9 ♗e3

When we got to this point, I vaguely recalled that it is strongly recommended for Black to stop the thematic d3-d4 advance preventing White from taking control of d4, among others.

9...♘d4 10 e5

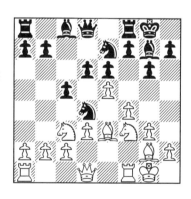

The sinister plot is finally revealed. This is the continuation he had in mind when he chose 6 f4. His gamble paid off as I had very little experience with this line because it's seen less often nowadays. I could not even remember ever studying it.

So what do we do when we are confronted with something unfamiliar in the opening? Do we cower in fear or regress in panic? If you answered "panic", consider switching to golf. Of course, we do neither. Instead, we bite our lip, furrow our brow and clench our fists for the ensuing fight.

10...♘ef5 11 ♗f2

Rybka attaches its standard annotation of "last book move" to White's eleventh because Black's next move is nowhere to be found in theory. It isn't there because it doesn't deserve a mention unless it is footnoted as a "bad" option. Afraid of White establishing a shuttle point on e4 for his knight into my position, I played ...d5 to contest the square, not caring for the cramping effect of the e-pawn.

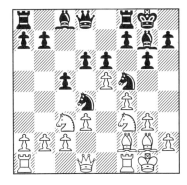

11...d5

11...♘xf3+ 12 ♕xf3 ♕b6 13 exd6

♕xb2 14 ♘e4 ♕xc2 15 ♖ac1 ♕xa2 16 ♖xc5 ♕a6 is a scary variation to get into because there are too many lines to calculate. The position is unclear, though I would prefer Black. Without any previous glimpse of this position in your study, you would never consider embarking on such a greedy path. This quality of preparation is infeasible for most adult amateurs given our other more pressing concerns like food on the table and a nagging boss. This intensity of preparation is the daily struggle of the professionals, but not ours. However, if you are eager for a new challenge, surprise yourself and embark on a journey to go as far as you can in the length of variations you consider on the board. Many of us really have no idea how deep we can go because we quit in the first instance of some fogginess or ambiguity in our calculations. Those who have tried tend to settle for the half-truths they find on the wayside and don't really strive for more. We also usually prefer the path which offers the least resistance. You know, we have a harsher word for it in our lingo; we call it laziness. But we embrace laziness with fewer qualms because the alternative means hard work.

It pays to make your brain hurt sometimes. Just try it at the very first opportunity that you can get, and you will find it liberating. Likewise, you will be merrily surprised with what you find. You will discover that fogginess like any fog slowly disappears over time. You will learn that pain in the brain hurts less and less as you do it more and more. And then, you will suddenly notice digital clarity. *Remember, extraordinary improvement will not come by ordinary efforts or feeble means.*

Another decent continuation for Black, endorsed by theory, is 11...♘xf3+ 12 ♕xf3 ♘d4 13 ♕d1 dxe5 14 fxe5 ♗xe5 15 ♘e4, a line I will likely use at the next opportunity. This brings to mind what GM Gurevich has repeatedly said to me in every manner possible, that one learns openings better and faster by merely playing them. I think he means that significant understanding of opening set-ups can only come during and after their employment. We learn certain information about certain lines by reading a book, but it is not until we gain over-the-board experience with it that we really learn in a more functional depth the essence of an opening line. I bet you, I am now better schooled at playing against 6 f4 of the Closed Sicilian, and better informed on the particular nuances associated with the 10 e5 line as well.

12 ♘xd4 ♘xd4 13 ♘e2

13 ♘b1 is weak and 13...b6 gives Black undeserved equality as Black gets to protect the c-pawn without any concession.

13...♘xe2+ 14 ♕xe2 ♕c7

This inaccurate and careless move was played hastily. 14...b6 is necessary

before it is rendered too late.

My young opponent took considerable time on his following move. One thing I noticed in his other games is his tendency to get into time trouble. His long think produced an unexpected but very interesting effort:

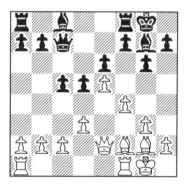

15 c4!? ♖d8

I considered 15...d4 but dismissed it because of 16 b4 cxb4 17 ♗xd4 ♖d8 18 ♕e4 when White's position is preferable – Black will have difficulty developing his queenside.

16 cxd5 exd5 17 ♖fc1 ♗f8

My last chance to play ...b6 comfortably was before this move. During the game I really felt my opponent's aggression. To his credit, he was trying everything to avoid a draw. This attitude didn't bother me a bit because I have learned from experience that unjustified attempts to win in a fairly even game usually backfire. I pacified my urge to strike back by telling myself to be patient and cautious, knowing that an opportunity to return fire would eventually present itself after

the aggressor overextended himself.
18 b4 b6 19 bxc5 bxc5 20 d4 c4

21 ♖xc4

White's previous committal moves led him to this scenario. If it works, then White is due his reward for being creative. Meanwhile, Black gets a passed pawn and a tempo to finally develop the light-squared bishop.

21...dxc4

21...♕xc4 22 ♕xc4 dxc4 23 ♗xa8 ♗f5 also deserves attention, with the idea of continuing with ...♗a3 to reach equality.

22 ♗xa8

Rybka analysis shows White as clearly better here. This means the compensation I thought I got with the passed pawn is given low regard by the chess engine. I worked with generalities reaching a flawed assessment; the engine relied on brute force calculations of concrete lines reaching a precise evaluation.

22...♗e6 23 ♗e4 c3

I wasted no time in pushing the passed pawn forward towards its coro-

nation. My hope to slow down White a bit resided in this push.

24 ♕f3

This move is inaccurate. A much better alternative is 24 ♕a6, which effectively paralyzes Black's queenside. More importantly, the queen on a6 prevents Black from deploying the bishop on a3 as in the game.

24...♗a3

I am proud of this move. I think it's the most accurate as it prevents White from advancing his a-pawn making a3 a better home for my dark-squared bishop. But more importantly it eyes the critical c1-square. The downside is allowing White's natural follow-up.

I could have prevented his next move with 24...♕a5 but declined the opportunity because I reckoned my passed pawn to be faster than his. Time pressure did not give either one of us the respite to prove or disprove with concrete moves our respective hunches.

25 d5

The less direct 25 ♖e1 ♗b2 26 ♗c2 leads to even chances.

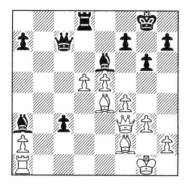

25...♗c8?

The bishop's misguided retreat yielded White an advantage, but to my relief he failed to exploit the gift. White should have continued after this inaccuracy with 26 d6 gaining a tempo on the queen and establishing control of d5.

Taking the advancing pawn with 25...♗xd5, which at the time both players deemed to be impossible, is Black's best chance to stay alive. As you can see, it is far better to rely only on concrete moves for truly establishing the soundness or unreliability of an idea than on general principles. If 26 ♗xd5 then 26...♗b2 leads to equality. If White continues with 27 ♖e1, Black has 27...c2 28 ♕b3 c1♕ 29 ♖xc1 ♗xc1 and he has the slightly better chances.

26 ♖e1 ♕a5 27 ♖d1

My opponent was under severe time pressure at this point. I think he had less than one minute and I had about three minutes.

27 d6 is not easy to find as you tend to be more attracted to moves with

threats in time pressure situations. We reason that a non-forcing move lacks clarity and does not require your opponent to think longer for a response. So we ignore it even though it could in fact be the best move on the board.

27...h5

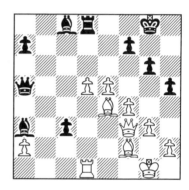

This motivated move was intended to exploit my opponent's time trouble and it worked. He had less than five seconds when he finally made his response. The 30-second increment became White's ally from here on.

27...♗b2 is to be preferred as it doesn't weaken the light squares around the king. But I could not resist making a threat.

28 ♖d4?

My game strategy of presenting my opponent with practical difficulties was forcing him to burn up precious seconds on his moves. He literally had two seconds left on his clock when he made this move, an inaccuracy. If he had more time, he would have found 28 ♕d3 ♔g7 29 e6 ♗xe6 30 ♗d4+ f6 31 ♗xc3, which would have put him clearly on top. Not good is 31 dxe6 ♖xd4 32 ♕e2 (32 ♕xd4?? ♗c5) 32...♖xd1+ 33 ♕xd1 ♕b6+ 34 ♔g2 ♕xe6 when it is Black who gets a slight edge.

28...♗g4

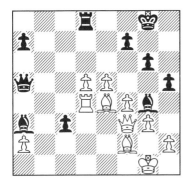

Black takes over the initiative. Suddenly the White queen is running out of squares.

29 ♕d3 ♗c5 30 e6

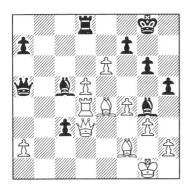

30...f5?

Both players were in serious time trouble at this point, with each side down to the last few seconds. The clock was having a seesaw effect on the advantage almost at each turn.

This move gives White the chance to get back in the game. The brave 30...fxe6 keeps the lead for Black. I rejected it because I was so afraid of 31 ♗xg6 and I had no time to calculate the lines. Play may continue as follows: 31...♗xd4 32 ♗h7+ ♔f8 33 ♕xd4 ♖xd5 34 ♕f6+ ♔e8 with Black having an undisputed edge. There was no way either player could assess this position correctly, even with more time.

31 ♗g2?

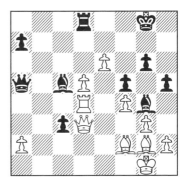

The tragedy of errors continues on both sides. We were pretty much just reacting to threats and simply avoiding serious blunders like hanging a piece. This is what happens when you disregard good time management practices. As a practical matter, in a game where there is a 30-second increment you must counter threats with your own bigger threats to force the other side to burn time. Forcing your opponent to change rhythm has a disconcerting effect especially in mutual time pressure.

An equalizing continuation for White is 31 e7 ♖e8 32 d6 fxe4 33 ♕xe4.

31...Rb8?

Not to be outdone, Black returns the favour and allows the opponent back into the game. Here I thought of taking the rook on d4 now, as in 31...Bxd4 32 Bxd4 c2 33 Qxc2 Qe1+ 34 Bf1 Bh3 35 Qe2 Qxf1+ 36 Qxf1 Bxf1 37 Kxf1 Rxd5 with advantage to Black.

32 d6

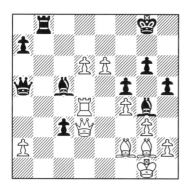

32...Bxd4?

The game is sadly turning into a blunderfest in which the player who makes the last mistake loses.

The greedy 32...Qxa2, ignoring the scary 33 d7, keeps Black fighting for winning chances with 33...Kh7. This is the type of steely move you want to be making in your games, but it is attainable only when you are looking judiciously at concrete moves. It disturbs me even now for not seeing it during the game.

33 Bxd4 c2

Black got stuck with this erroneous plan hatched earlier, and seeing that I had nothing else, my last move was tossed in as a bluff.

34 Be3?

Well, almost any bluff can work in time pressure. With the simple 34 Qxc2, White is winning: 34...Qb4 35 Be5 Qe1+ 36 Bf1 will no longer work because White's passed pawns will be unstoppable.

34...Qe1+ 35 Bf1

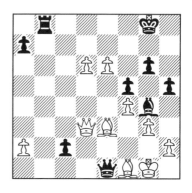

35...c1Q?

Completely winning is 35...Bh3. In fact, it was the idea behind the 33...c2 bluff. But seeing that White erred in not taking the pawn one move earlier, I thought I might as well promote it and get a piece out of it. I also incorrectly assumed that the line would simply transpose, but it turned out Black had no time to delay the ...Bh3 plan.

After 35...Bh3 White could try to confuse Black with 36 d7 threatening to queen next move with check (if 36 Qe2 then 36...Rb1 37 Qxe1 Rxe1 wins), but again the simple 36...Kh7 brings home the point: White cannot promote with 37 d8Q because of 37...Rxd8 and White cannot recapture on d8 with 38 Qxd8 as Black mates with 38...Qxf1.

I would probably have seen 36...♔h7 had I gone into this line as necessity is often known to breed good moves.

36 ♗xc1 ♕xc1 37 d7 ♕c5+ 38 ♔h1 ♕e7

A similar idea to ...♔h7 and equally potent is 38...♔g7, which avoids any check on the eighth rank. Play might continue as in the line 39 h3 ♖d8 40 hxg4 ♕c6+ 41 ♔h2 ♕xe6 42 gxf5 ♕xd7 43 ♕c3+ ♕d4 44 ♕c7+ ♖d7 with Black having a winning advantage.

39 h3

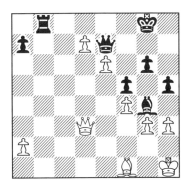

I overlooked this nice resource. I really thought White's game should end in resignation. The loss of the extra piece hardly changes the outcome as Black is still winning, but the emotional letdown and many near-time forfeits were beginning to take their toll.

The rest of the game is given with only light comments.

39...♗f3+ 40 ♕xf3 ♕xe6 41 ♕d3 ♖d8 42 ♕c4 ♔f7 43 ♕xe6+ ♔xe6 44 ♗c4+

♔d6 45 ♗b5 ♔c5 46 ♗a4 ♔d6 47 ♔g2 ♔e7 48 g4 h4 49 gxf5 gxf5 50 ♔f3

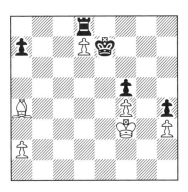

50...♖xd7??

Black's position was so dominating that I failed to notice the simple 50...♖g8 when, as most annotators would now say, the rest is a simple matter of technique.

But after White' recapture on d7, it dawned on me that I had just blundered a win into a draw.

51 ♗xd7 ♔xd7 52 ♔e3 ♔c6 53 ♔d4 ♔d6 54 ♔c4 ♔c6 55 ♔d4 ♔d6 56 a3 a6 57 ♔c4 ♔c6 ½-½

Winning positions are simply just that, unless they are brought to conclusion. You can never relax until your opponent resigns or checkmate is delivered.

My young opponent finally earned his first IM norm in this series, in July 2009.

Conclusion

What else do you need besides the chess thinking process and the improvement plan laid out in this book? First and foremost, you must be equipped with the right attitude. Self-belief is a necessary ingredient in chess warfare. By right attitude I mean your overall attitude with regards to who you are in relation to the game. The one who thinks he can improve is the one who does. It is simply that.

The opposite is even truer because no improvement is easy to achieve. You simply do nothing and you are already there. Nobody improves by inertia. Status quo stunts improvement and often leads to regression. Those who improve the least are those who quit trying. Our inabilities or failures in chess are mostly accounted for by our lack of effort. If you say that you can no longer improve in chess then you will likely not. Saying you are a player who is prone to blunders and accepting that as your fated lot is a dangerous road you do not want to be on. If defeatism describes your attitude, I am certain your success in that regard will come to you swiftly. You will be adept in numbing your heartaches when blunders occur. When you begin to accept mediocrity, it quickly becomes your highest achievement.

Second, modify or replace your current chess thinking process. The state of disrepair in your abilities is indicative of something amiss in your chess thinking process. It cannot be fixed by simply mending the current process. It has to be replaced with a new one.

Third, you must commit to the uniform application of the chess thinking process rigidly until the desired proficiency is achieved. Elsewhere in the book I said that effort makes a big difference, especially the right kind of effort. Also, you must tailor the process to your strengths and weaknesses. The process must become as natural as your breathing to become most effectual. Your success will come faster after you have assimilated and internalized the process so that it becomes second nature to you. But never forget that any improvement process no matter how efficient by definition must continually change.

Do not be discouraged when you see a noticeable lag in your experience between chess improvement and rating. Any gains in rating are ultimately a function of chess improvement, which are gains both in chess knowledge and chess skill. Stay focussed on improving and your rating will eventually catch up confirming its undeniable presence. Meanwhile, find motivation in your improving results against stronger opposition and the decreasing incidence of blunders in your game.

I now invite you to join me in the quest for lasting chess improvement at any age. Wise up and become an improving player. Please email me at rook@USMilitaryChess.org your comments, questions and suggestions with regards to the chess thinking process dissected above. Do not hesitate to share your personal struggles either from the application of your own chess thinking process or from the amalgamation of systems including the one championed by this writer. If you decide to give my system a try and as a positive outcome you see some qualified success in your play, please tell me so we can give it due mention in future follow-up articles.

On a personal note, I am giving myself three years to achieve the FIDE Master title. By then, I will be 50. When that happens, you will see another book. Mind you, I have already decided on a title. Wish me well.

Wishing you good chess,
Andres D. Hortillosa
Improving Player

Index of Openings

Figures refer to page numbers

Index of Games